Wounded Song

Wounded Song

Wounded Song

When you're left to wade through
the aftermath of abuse,
it begs the question,
"Now What?"

Tammy Sue Willey 2017

© 2017
By Tammy Sue Willey

Scripture quotations marked NIV are taken from the Holy Bible, New International Version®, NIV® Copyright © 1973, 1978, 1984, 2011 by Biblica, Inc.® Used by permission. All rights reserved worldwide.

Scripture references marked NIV are taken from the Holy Bible, New International Version®, NIV® Copyright © 1973, 1978, 1984, 2011 by Biblica, Inc.® Used by permission. All rights reserved worldwide.

Scripture quotations marked *The Message* are taken from *The Message by Eugene H. Peterson,* copyright © 1993, 1994, 1995, 1996, 2000, 2001, 2002. Used by permission of NavPress Publishing Group.

Consulting Editor: Bronwyn Petry
Cover design: Dawn Barrett
Cover photo – front: 1973 Violin Lessons
Cover photo – back: 2015 Violin Lessons
Author's photo: Calf's Creek Utah
Interior Photos: Family Archive
Illustrations: Tammy Sue Willey

Memoir: It's my story through the eyes of my memory coupled with shared family references, stories and letters. Real names used, alive, gave me permission. Characters are not made up, but some names have been changed to respect privacy. Also read Epigraph and Preface.

Blog: woundedsong.com   Email: admin@woundedsong.com
Blog: tammysuewilley.blogspot.com
Facebook: Change Your View, Change Your World…one step at a time

ISBN-13: 978-1548536343
ISBN-10: 1548536342

Wounded Song

ENCOURAGEMENT ALONG THE WAY

"This was brutal-yet amazing. What a story. I am hooked. I feel it in my gut. I feel the pain of the scared little girl that I just want to take into my arms and hug tightly and protect from this terrible nightmare." *and then the food...*
"Issues around food-so wrong-how amazing that it didn't lead to an eating disorder, but then, I don't know maybe it did? What a cruel thing to have done." Chapter: A Bowl of Onions. J.G. married mother, middle school French teacher. Connecticut November 2016

"Tammy Sue ... I have been crying on and off all morning finishing your book. I can't find the words for on how many different levels it touched me. It's amazing, brilliant and purely heartfelt. I cannot wait to have a copy someday. Reading it has forever changed me in a way that is so powerful." Gayle H.
Marlborough, CT July 2016

"This will help women. This story has to be out there. You're not preaching, it's from your heart." Excerpts from: The Twig Snapped, Bowl of Onions and Dust Returns to the Ground. Admin. Coordinator/Private School, friend D.D. Farmington, CT. June 2013

"Wow! Your whole story needs to be out there." Chapter: The Fragile Dance. Reverend Barbara.
Glastonbury, CT June 2013

"Your book got me thinking, even if you weren't abused, one could relate to aspects of your story. I could also relate to the Mother's Day card dilemma and my mother-daughter relationship with my mom." Retired registered nurse, Manchester, CT March 30, 2016

"I finished your incredibly amazing book. I have so many different ways to view it. The amount of similarities in our lives is overwhelming! When I came east to visit, I had one question I wanted to ask a male friend, 'How long does it take to find peace with your father when he is dead?' I never got the chance to ask him, but after reading your draft, your book gave me my answer." Betty Ann Smith Houston, Texas September 2013

"Ms. Willey has written a memoir that comes straight from *her* heart and will touch *your* heart like no other book can. She writes from a raw emotion that connects with her readers on a primal level. I highly recommend this book. If you've been abused, or even if you haven't, you'll find a nugget in Tammy Sue's story that will make you cry, laugh or contemplate your own life while relating to hers."
Linda Peterson Loegel, mother of the author.
North Carolina December 2016

"Wow, what beautiful writing. Raw and Honest. I hear words with imagery. It doesn't feel constructed." She read the Introduction, I Hit My Head and Cried and random excerpts. Friend T.B., public school, married mom of two. Coventry, CT. June 2013

"When I re-read the chapter A Bowl of Cherries, I felt my heart rate go up as I read the words. I knew the ending, but as I'm laying here reading this today as an adult, I swear I was back on that twin bed trembling? Dawn N. Barrett, best friend, married, mother of three.
Sandy Hook, CT November 2016

"I really admire your courage Tammy Sue. Writing a book and baring your soul is not easy. However, what a gift you have given to yourself and others. You are a very talented writer. Thank you for sharing your life with all of us. I have gained new insight and perspective about some of the struggles you and I have endured." Nancy Meyer, cousin. Registered nurse, married and mother of one.
Watertown, CT November 2016

"So proud of what you've accomplished. As you know I've not read any excerpts so I can't honestly give a review. All I can say is I anxiously await to hold a finished copy in my hands. I know that in everything you do, there is a blending of God, warmth, honesty, compassion, well-being, nurturing and so much more than can be put into words. Love you sis, your brother, Michael." Father, brother and son.
Seymour, CT October 2016

"Just finished reading your chapter The Fragile Dance. Amazing! I just want to cry! My husband and I can relate to your story, how we both came from wounded relationships after a long time of not being in one." Newlywed Connecticut Couple, D.N. runs vocational mentor program.
Connecticut September 2014

"I love my cousin Tammy. I love the determination you have to work through the tough relationship issues. Say what needs saying, ask what needs asking. I know it's probably difficult for you yet you are better than most of us at it." Bobby, cousin, Engineer, married father of two. Woodstock, CT September 2016

The question to the reader was: "After you read my book, did it feel disrespectful to my family dead and alive?" Her answer: "You did an amazing job of speaking the truth without indicting anyone. As you matured you stood outside looking in at this cast of characters. We could not have done that. It was a long journey for you but you, with God, you were victorious." Aunt Dee.
Fairfield, CT. March 2014

Wounded Song is such a great title to this labor of love. Our lives are an orchestration of events and emotions which inspire decisions we make either in the here and now or in the future. As you read Tammy Sue's story, you'll see how she masterfully combines pain and healing. This read will tug at your heart both for the hurt soul and for the forgiving spirit. There comes a point in our lives when we realize harboring unforgiveness only hurts ourselves. Tammy Sue's story reminds us of that fact and shows no matter how deep the wound is, it is still our choice to forgive and that it can be done.
Little Shadow, happily married grandma.
North Carolina December 2016

DEDICATED

To my husband, my mom, sister, brother and family and
all the Jenna's and Zayda-Lyn's of the world
fighting for their life story.

Be determined to break any chains that may bind and blind
so numbness doesn't win. Your unique light was designed
for you to share.

He brought them out of darkness, the utter darkness,
and broke away their chains.
Psalm 107:14

The light shines in the darkness,
and the darkness has not overcome it.
John 1:5

EPIGRAPH

"Home is where my story began. A wall of family photos reveals much, but sometimes that wall hides the untold story. I don't expect family to remember events the way I do because the timeline of our family growth and family decay unfolded differently for each. While the culture of our familial traits helped to shape us all, our individual stories remain unique and personal." Tammy Sue Willey

Wounded Song

CONTENTS

Wounded Song

FOREWORD

by Betty Ann Smith, Houston, Texas May 2017

Ever need the answer to that deep dark question held in your hopeless envelope? I did.

My personal and desperate need led me back east where it all began. I arranged a rendezvous with an old soul mate I hadn't seen in forty years. I knew only he could be trusted with the answer to my question. I prayed for the chance to walk around the block with him and ask, "How long does it take to find peace with your abuser, your father, when he is dead?"

On the 3 ½ hour flight east I allowed the words of the song "Like A Rolling Stone," to replay over and over in my head; a song which had been dedicated to me when I last saw my abuser, my father.

The GPS led me from the airport to a small New England town I was all too familiar with. Heading for my friend's house, I made a right turn onto a little dead end street which brought me to his yellow 1879 colonial house with picket fence, old gnarled trees, and garden beds bursting with color. How perfect I thought as my heart became calm. I knew then, that God led me here for my rebirth.

Armed with my God wink and calm in my heart, I knocked at the back door. The door unlatched and there stood, not my soul mate, but Tammy Sue Willey with long red wavy hair, loving blue eyes, and arms opened for my immediate hug. After a beautiful dinner and caught-up conversations, I knew I was home.

Tammy Sue, a complete stranger, wife of the man I trusted with my soul, shared her beautiful girl room, a safe sanctuary from pain and suffering for women, including herself; a place safe from past abusers. After spending a little time there, and getting to know each other, I realized I finally felt visible and my life was about to look different.

When we said our good byes, she handed me a 300-page book marked draft-5 for me to take on the 3 ½ hour plane ride home. Little did I know this manuscript would take me on the journey of my life.

As I reflected on the visit with my soul mate and his wife, I began to read her book about the oldest child of an abusive alcoholic father who was married to her church going mother. Still air bound, I shared the pain of Tammy Sue's upbringing as I read from cover to end. Only this time a different song replayed over and over in my head, "One of Us."

I identified with Tammy Sue as the target of this 1960s family. After all, children were starving in China so she was forced to eat garbage scraps. She was met with consistent degrading remarks such as, *it's your fault, you'll be nothing, you're fat,* and lived in fear of when the clock struck 6:00 p.m., the time to return to that dinner table. She had placed me in the chair next to her and transported me back to when I had been told many of the same things and more.

Tammy Sue shares her childhood perspective of her undeveloped family and life after *him.* She walks and hides from her adolescence to young adulthood and beyond in fear, intimidation, criticism, physical and emotional abuse. The result of this abuse made it all the more difficult to navigate relationships, her genetic disorder and an empty womb. Left barren, she wrestles with the inability to keep the promise to herself to break the cycle. Her story details the power of abuse along the road of torment. Even in death, it ultimately leads to the impossible question, "Now What?"

Her question made me face my deepest dark question, "How long does it take to find peace with your abuser, your father?" Her book completed my walk around the block. The walk I never had with my soul mate, because his wife answered my question.

I encourage you to walk with her so you too, can find your song.

Self-portrait of Betty Ann 1973

Credentials ~ A lived life experience ~
"I totally understand this book because
I'm a child of that era
and suffered through a lot of the same."

PREFACE

I wrote this memoir to help others. It is based on my personal experience and memories coupled with family input to clarify certain details. In addition to my account of how a conversation(s) went, there is some dialogue that represents the character and nature of either my experience or what was shared with me, of that person. In addition to my personal experience, my story, much of the information within is public record; vital statistics, funerals, headstones and newspaper articles.

Nor was this written in haste. I labored over my story for years. The intent of this book has never been to hurt anyone, dead or alive. Rather, its goal has been an effort to help and encourage those who may be stuck in their wound while offering another view in kindness.

Once the initial sting of abuse is over and one is left to wade through the aftermath, it begs the question, "Now What?"

INTRODUCTION

I believe in the depth of our soul there is a life song that sings our stories, which swell to our surface seeking joyous release. It reminds us we are alive and that the art of us was created for the purpose of sharing the message within. But we must beware, for there is an invisible enemy anxious to squash our story and snuff out our light.

God only knows the topic of abuse isn't original. So what would I gain by exposing the 30 year-old dirty laundry I'm supposed to hide? It occurred to me I was wounded and I no longer wanted to remain enslaved to the emotional confusion of my past. Perhaps what I'd gain is freedom from the lies of the abuse.

Do-gooders threw many platitudes my way which added to my confusion; "time heals all wounds," "forgive," and "honor your parents." You're kidding right? Forgive the abuse and honor the person who beat me and the one who stayed quiet? Seriously? Aren't I allowed to be angry? Cry? Grieve? Give the silent treatment? It's not my fault that I was abused.

The family photo album puzzled me. It appeared filled with love because of the many pictures and smiles, but was void of those showing the alcoholic parent or the silence of the other one who never said anything. The pictures could not show the dark cloud on a sunny day or the heaviness of the air in our home.

Further confused by the album, I even questioned my childhood memories of abuse. I have hazy recounts of a young girl who began to discover and express herself with imagination. I saw her drawing and playing the violin but then she struggled to talk, to sing, to dance, to create, and to be. Did I imagine the strain and harsh tones that left me flat and silent?

Once an adult, I decided not all the family photos were bad. They just did not always tell the whole story. Therefore, I yearned to be freed from the groaning I heard in the pit of my soul; a groaning which began as a whimper in need of being uncovered, unwrapped and unstuck.

While I searched for answers, the Conductor of my soul waited with patience for me so He could begin the next verse of my life song in order to "...protect me from trouble and surround me with songs of deliverance."[1]

Like it or not, all will have a familial experience to go through, but how we come out the other end will be up to us. In the midst of the fight hold steadfast because our life song fosters in us a hope that wants to help us shine.

ONE

Tavern Bench

Alone in the dining room with Dad, I stared. I couldn't help myself. I mean, after all these years Dad was here in our house. When he arrived a few weeks ago, my husband of sixteen years met him for the first time. Dad had missed out on much of my growing years and became absent during my adulthood. He missed our wedding day, musical jam parties and many dinner opportunities. Really what he missed was everyday life stuff. But here he was now for this long-overdue visit, in our house for the first time. I thought, *it's better late than never so be thankful he's here.* But then I thought, *where were you when I needed you?* I gazed around the room soaking in this unexpected reunion when a sense of peace washed over me.

From the dining room chair, I looked at the black box Dad came with as he sat on the brown tavern bench my husband had found at a local yard sale. Unlike my childhood days, we sat still and quiet together.

Amused I asked, "What am I going to do with you?"

Curious to have this one-on-one moment with Dad, I pondered the heaviness of his dead body inside the black box and wondered how much he weighed. How heavy could ashes be? It's funny how something this dead, not a little dead, or kind of dead, but dead dead fills a little six-by-nine inch box and without muttering a word can erupt a lifetime of questions and memories to my surface. Personal stories that had been interrupted, stuffed and left for dead. Stories

1

from long ago, that had surrendered to the end of their season, now gasped for air, hoping to be revived.

I could resuscitate the old stories that were looking to put a stranglehold on me or I could let the box remind me of how far I've come and be determined to live my life alive. The box that held my dad brought me to the middle of my crossroad. The choice I make will be mine.

TWO

I Hit My Head and Cried

My bones felt tense when I sat at my desk in our guest room. I wasn't sure why. Nothing specific happened, yet so many things had happened. But I wasn't dwelling on them. It was called life. Wasn't it? It's not like I could put a finger on it but I had grown tense and out of sorts. Was it something that happened yesterday or was it because my second husband and I sold our photo business years earlier when film changed to digital? Maybe I didn't like being a statistic from a failed marriage. Perhaps it was because my father had been an alcoholic and no matter what I did or didn't do as a child I couldn't lock into the good girl formula. Neither parent had seemed satisfied. One was drunk and bitter while the other remained silent. Or maybe I was having an off day because when I was sixteen, tests confirmed I carried Dad's genetic disease of hemophilia. A disorder that would give my future daughter a fifty-fifty chance of carrying on the family strain, or worse my future son might be like my dad. Wow! The voice of my fear declared that should I get pregnant, the baby I carried would grow into an angry, bitter, and abusive man. On the other hand it's possible the tension was clinging to our infertility. Or was it just because of the crib?

Attempting to organize my desk, I dropped a piece of cardboard on the floor. When I crawled under the desk to grab it I whacked my head on the keyboard tray. It hurt. I cried. I leaned on my elbows under the desk and watched

3

tears drip onto the plastic chair mat. I noticed they weren't clear like the mat.

I didn't cry because my head hurt, I cried because my hurt hurt. I've become sensitive to random thoughts. Not sure why, but I have my theory. God. I don't mean God is doing it to me; whatever it is. But because I try hard to do life God's way with a greater awareness of Him, it seems an unidentified force has intercepted my efforts and pecks at me. Peck, peck, peck. Not one big thing. Not one little thing, rather many gradual peck, peck, pecks that goad me to find my last straw and throw in the towel.

Another drop fell, this time on the piece of cardboard that started this whole mess. I watched my tear turn dark brown as the thickness absorbed my cry, spreading random inkblot patterns. I sobbed. I felt silly. I wanted to shout. I thought, maybe this is like the stories I've heard. When one is hurt and driven to their knees, God comes, maybe even sends an Angel. But then the voice in my head said, "You foolish girl, how contrived if you can already picture the scene of your hope." So rather, than shout out loud for my God to help, I whispered as I tried to ignore the mocking voice in my head. Yet my heart still silently hoped for an angel to appear and set me straight, but one never came.

> ...rather than
> shout loud for my God
> to help, I whispered...

My body released its history of hurts into a salty discolored puddle under the desk. I cried out I know God will be there, I know He has a plan, I know He won't hang me out to dry. I know, I know, I know, but if I know, why do I hurt?

THREE

The Turkey Baster

A thin cotton hospital sheet drapes over my body and hangs off the edge of the exam table in an environment screaming sterile. With my husband by my side, we look at each other and ask, "Was it good for you too?" Holding hands, we laugh. The only thing missing is a cigarette, but we don't smoke.

Well, there was more missing, privacy. I mean, this was like year three or four of our infertility process. Within a delicate time-frame, we needed to acquire my husband's sperm. This interlude could take place at home on a timed schedule according to my ovulation clock. Without hesitation we'd put the collection into a sterilized cup, stick it in a bag to conceal the effort and then drive like crazed people to the medical facility, presenting our bagged future to the girl behind the window. Trying to start a family doesn't get more romantic than this!

If we wanted to avoid the added anxiety of driving across the river into the city through all kinds of weather and highway traffic while not damaging the goods, the medical facility offered private rooms where my husband and I could accommodate one another in our effort to collect his sperm and conceive a child. This room was a small lounge with a couch, chair, television and a table strewn with magazines for our entertainment. I felt like I was in the lobby of a cheap motel. The couch provided to us was made of some washable synthetic material. I couldn't afford to imagine we weren't the first couple to ever utilize this room so a part of me shut down.

When I heard voices and footsteps on the other side of the door I was reminded this wasn't our home but rather a medical office. There was, of course, no pressure. Once convinced we weren't on candid camera, we accomplished our romantic endeavor. I'm not sure what part of this process might've been considered foreplay.

Our hopeful heir was collected and put in the plastic sterile bottle provided for easy delivery. After handing it to the nameless face at the counter, its contents were then put through a process the doctors called washing. We were privileged to watch our maybe-child have its first bath. Once deemed clean, our future was put into a long syringe, which we dubbed the turkey baster. We were then ushered into a room which replicated my annual OB/GYN appointment. They covered me with an ugly oversized shirt with one tie string that never stayed tied. Not one stitch of this huge drab shirt offered sexy lingerie appeal; it refused to glide against my body like a soft silk teddy. Rather it draped over me like a hand-me-down stiff cotton sheet as my feet were placed in the cold metal stirrups. Once I assumed the position, the doctor stuck the turkey baster in me and ejected my husband's sperm. Great! This has now become a threesome. What little dignity we had left from our not-so-romantic interlude evaporated as the doctor left the room. My husband and I basked in the glow of maybe this time.

Illustration: *If you tell me to relax one more time, I'll have to seriously hurt you!*

On the heels of me saying we couldn't get pregnant, I was ready to punch the next person who told me to just relax, as they recounted story after story about someone they knew who conceived because they weren't trying so hard.

If one more person asked if we were going to adopt, I'd scream. And if I had to hear yet another story about somebody who knew somebody who became pregnant after they adopted, as if adopting was the only answer for one's loss, well, I didn't know what I was going to do. Probably cry again.

Would you tell a person who recently lost their spouse you have a blind date lined up for them, or a woman who lost her baby, she can have another? In the immediacy of the wound, the fact was we were grieving the loss of our own unmet natural dreams.

Although I wanted to scream, it occurred to me most well-meaning people feel helpless. Their heart-felt advice comes freely, like casseroles at a funeral. It is their way of offering help and hope to my hurt.

Illustration: *If I wanted to adopt, I'd say I'm adopting. Right now, I'm infertile.*

I learned there is no formula to how or when one grieves their loss. And when they are ready to forgive the loss, they will choose whether to adopt or to marry. The wounds and the choices are personal.

Stressed? Try not to be stressed: when fun and intimacy are taken out of what should be fun and intimate. Not so easy when everything I did revolved around my menstrual cycle, which worked like clockwork, and when after practicing on oranges, I had to give myself shots in the stomach. CAT scans and MRIs were ordered to rule out the possibility of having a tumor on my brain stem. No stress there. After a series of blood tests, I fell into the small-unexplained-percentage of infertile women who couldn't get pregnant.

Illustration: *Stressed? Why should I be stressed? Basil temp, hormone shots, dye shots, blood lab, put husband on calendar, sex via petri dish, doctor body invasions, and pregnant stories. What Stress?*

Every month I was reminded I'm a woman by my cycle. Yet every month the lack of conception reminded me I wasn't a mother. Coupled with the routine of basal temperatures, hormone shots, timed-sex, blood tests and more doctor appointments, aware or not, you bet I was stressed!

Still lying on the table holding my husband's hand, we hope this time our sperm and egg dance so our future son or daughter will be conceived.
Again ... no dance.

Through the five plus years of trying to conceive, there'd been many tears and many prayers. During the peak of our infertility process, when emotions were raw and tears flowed like rivers, every time I turned around somebody my age or older was getting pregnant followed by baby showers and dedications.

I had dreamed of being a mom in the neighborhood; the kind who had an open door available to any wayward kid looking for a hug, a home-baked cookie, or somewhere safe.

During my first marriage, our vows melted my fear of having children so I collected framed teddy bear pictures, a wind-up carousel music box, unicorns and random knick-knacks for a little child's room.

The Christmas tree skirt I made had seasonal colors and hand-sewn candy canes in each corner. Oh, it was nothing fancy, but I put it aside as my first quilt for a crib.

But then we went from baby talk to divorce.

Married again, my new husband and I desired to be parents.

Like a garden in need of fresh soil and vegetation, we yearned for something tender to sprout. We tried and tried to plant a new seed. But years of infertility squashed that blossom.

Yet hope always appeared when I timed my monthly shots perfectly after practicing on oranges. My cycle was late. Someone older than me gave birth. Someone at the ice cream stand by the beach announced, after years of trying, she was pregnant for the first time.

Hope wavered when I heard yet, another story about how I should relax. And eventually hope faded as my monthly cycle refused to line up with my husband's business trips. Nor was it revived when we accidentally applied a spermicidal gel which killed off all efforts. Well, we didn't know, the packaging looked like the other tube.

Once during this fruitless escapade, and running on fumes, I walked into the Morning Glory antique shop on Main Street. Hidden in the back corner was an old white crib on little metal wheels. The decorative oval tin attached to the outside of the head board displayed a raised metal rabbit.

How perfect. Not only charming, but vintage.

Our 1879 home would welcome this new addition.

Immediately I felt connected to the crib and alive again.

Hope re-entered.

Maybe this meant I was relaxed.

My husband supported my desire to purchase it. "Whatever you wanna do," he said.

I drove to the store several times.

Hemmed and hawed over the contraption that called me.

Dreamed.

Imagined.

I tried to justify the purchase because we weren't pregnant yet.

However, determined to have this, I paced back and forth.

"How silly," the voice in my head said. "What are you gonna do with this if you don't have a baby?"

"Put dolls in it."

"What dolls?" the voice said.

"I'll buy them."

"How silly," the voice chided.

"Okay, my stuffed animals."

"What, those old, musty, ancient artifacts from your robbed childhood?"

Maybe the voice was right.

Buy an antique crib just to cram it with old stuffed fiber? That's not practical.

Drowning in logic, I went back to the Morning Glory to dispute the conflict.

I walked to the back corner room one last time but I couldn't find the crib.

The clerk, now familiar with me announced, "It's not back there, I sold it yesterday."

Back home I cried.

If only I hadn't wavered.

Why didn't I just buy the stupid crib?

If only I hadn't stopped hoping.

Is that why we didn't get pregnant?

Well, how much power does a silly ole' crib have over my womb anyway?

I cannot fix what I cannot fix. Soon after, the dated knick-knacks and the corny Christmas tree quilt found their way to the local thrift stores.

It seemed so unfair when I watched people have child after child with little effort. I felt that my God was testing the aching of my womb.[2]

No longer certain of my desires, I began to doubt I'd be a good mother. Maybe God thinks I'd be a lousy one. Maybe I'm being punished. People often liken their relationship with God to that of their earthly father so what else am I to think?

I reflected on my childhood when I had vowed never to have children or be like my parents. I had prayed for the family patterns of abuse to be stopped. Was being infertile my answered prayer? Did this mean I would have continued the abuse? Would I have been violent or silent? What about my husband? He loses, too. Were my prayers creating his loss when we were both looking to be loved and renewed? Were the sins of my father spilling over into our marriage?

I was sorrowful and confused.

Random baby dedications could take place during any given Sunday church service and most times I'd be happy for the new family. Yet without warning, a Sunday dedication could open the floodgates of loss.

In addition to these peaks and valleys at church, Mother's Day became a dreaded man-made holiday for me. Inevitably, on this special day, several proud parents would line up at the front of the sanctuary eager to have their newborns dedicated. One by one, as babies were held up for the congregation to see, the moms glowed while I shut down.

Following one particular Mother's Day, the Pastor rattled off glowing attributes of motherhood. After the syrup was poured, he topped his sundae sermon with a cherry that said, "So come on ladies let's get busy and have more babies." Ouch! His verbal blow punched me in the gut right where all my womanhood had failed me.

How could our pastor be so insensitive? Doesn't he know that not every woman is a mother and not everyone has a good relationship with their mother? There are many layers to the scars of motherhood beyond the stretch marks and obvious duty stated on a Hallmark card. For the same reason I couldn't get on the bandwagon of political correctness with a well-intentioned friend who was only insensitive in a kind way, was the same reason I couldn't rebuke our Pastor.

After much consideration, I realized, rather than taking people to task, most people reach out from their heart with an innate desire to make another's situation better. They may fumble, but I believe their intent is to try to help, not hurt.

Through this painful process and while listening to advice, I had time to wonder how many people I had hurt with unsolicited words. I still make mistakes but I'm learning to pause before shooting off my mouth.

However, I also learned if I have to over-think every time I want to aid, help, share, love, show compassion, or lend an ear to a friend, then I might as well do nothing.

Albeit unintentional, at some point I will say the wrong thing and hurt somebody's feelings because what is sensitive to them is not to me for I haven't walked in their shoes.

I discovered through my own pain that I am heightened to my own story. Rather than become selfish and claim the church and whole world should tiptoe around me, I learned to set my own boundaries. I decided I didn't need to go to church on Mothers' Day.

> I am heightened to
>
> my own story

Unfortunately, one particular Sunday morning I had yet to set those boundaries. At the peak of my emotional crumbling, the New England stoic in me walked out of the sanctuary when another baby was dedicated, but not until the scene unfolded in slow orchestration as the Pastor introduced a proud couple who held their precious little gift.

The mother's intense gaze at her baby girl struck a chord deep in me. From those depths churned the vignette of a life I imagined could have happened to me once upon a time. Glassy eyed and no longer in control of my tears, I tried one last time to conceal my loss as the battle poured down my face. I wanted to scream, *May you always look at your little girl like that. May you never waver at your responsibility and obligation to teach,*

> At the peak of
>
> my emotional
>
> crumbling

protect, and love this precious gift of life God has given to you.

The baby girl they held, only months old, had red hair much like me at her tender age. The mother's look in those split seconds provoked in me a sense of loss. I grieved not only for the child we couldn't conceive, but for the undying protection I had longed for from my mother many years ago.

FOUR

Before There Was Me

August 9, 1961

As the saying goes, boy meets girl. They fall in love.

Whirlwind romance.

The plan is to live happily ever after!

What girl doesn't want a fairy tale wedding where the magic of the moment lasts forever and his eyes always hold her like the first time they met?

Before there was me, there was them, my parents-to-be, John and Linda. Linda, about to turn twenty-one, thought she'd be an old maid spinster the remainder of her life. Fate had other plans. August of 1961 she went to a gathering at a girlfriend's house where she was introduced to John. My soon-to-be-parents were acquainted that evening when John whisked Linda off her feet with conversation and a smile which suggested John must be the one.

Linda, of English heritage, was from Springfield, Vermont.

John, half Italian and half Danish, was from Bridgeport, Connecticut.

Cultures apart they fell in love.

Two weeks after their blind date, Linda kept her planned vacation and traveled to Florida. In her absence John pined for Linda through the love letter[3] he wrote in 1961 which to this day Linda holds among her keepsakes with nostalgic fondness.

Page I

8-29-61
It's me
Hi Honey!

How are you? Did you enjoy your trip down to Florida.

I hope you had an enjoyable ride down and I hope it'll be the same for you coming back.

You know something sweets, I missed you the five days you were gone. Why did I have to meet you anyway?

I

*If I didn't know you
then I feel like I do any-
other day. "Terrible".
You know what? I'm glad
I feel this way.*

*Any how I have one thing
to look forward to —
You coming home.*

*I never was going to get
involved with another girl
like this ~~to~~ again, but I dont
know how to stop it and now
I dont want to stop it, even if
I end up on the bottom. —*

Page II

If I didn't know you then I feel like I do any other day. "Terrible". You know what? I'm glad I feel this way.

Any how I have one thing to look forward to – you coming home.

I never was going to get involved with another girl like this again, but I don't know how to stop it an now I don't want to stop it, even if I end up on the bottom.

19

III

But honey, if you think that you might get hunt then quit now, befor it gets to much harder for you to.

Some guy I am, instead of trying to make you feel good all I'm doing is making you feel miserable.

How has the weather down there been for you?

Good, I hope.

I all most had to work Sat. But I changed days with the guy I work with.

Page III

But honey, if you think that you might get hurt then quit now, before it gets to much harder for you to.

Some guy I am, instead of trying to make you feel good all I'm doing is making you feel miserable.

How has the weather down there been for you?

Good, I hope.

I all most had to work Saturday but I changed days with the guy I work with.

IV

> It rained up here Sat, a Sun,
> off and on.
>
> Mon. and today have
> been good.
>
> That is, as good as it
> Could be, with out you here.
>
> Then I go again
> So far this week has
> been going by fast; thank
> God for that.
>
> I was up to Johnny's Sat, a
> Sun. So that helped. to night
>
> I was working on my car.
> Right now I am trying to

Page IV

It rained up here Saturday and Sunday off and on.

Monday and today have been good. That is, as good as it could be without you here.

There I go again.

So far this week has been going by fast, thank God for that.

I was up to Johnny's Saturday and Sunday so that helped tonight. I was working on my car.

Right now I am trying to...

Page V

...*write you a half way decent letter.*

How am I doing?

*I wish you were here so that I could talk to you that's
better than writing.*

*Have a good time will you and forget about me
till you come home ok.*

I will see you at the airport.

Your ever loving John xxxxxxxx
P.S. Don't be afraid when you come in

Linda's new beau, a self-taught musician, had an ear for playing guitar, much like her dad, a self-taught musician with an ear for the fiddle.

As a rule neither John nor Linda were raised in church or as church-goers for that matter, but the concept wasn't foreign to them. For their nuptials, John desired to be married in a Baptist church he had attended on a few occasions so they went as a couple to a few Sunday services to get to know the minister. Linda wanted to take her white gloves off to show her engagement ring but John told her that wasn't proper.

Cleaved together in marriage, their vows under God as their witness, the newlyweds purchased their first home, a 1940s trailer. All three rooms came furnished with built in drawers and highly polished solid wood walls. Life was grand for this newly-wed couple still in the glow of their honeymoon bliss. John called his bride, sweets, milk was delivered to the door and they named their puppy Schotzie. They'd race to the table top Christmas tree to see who'd be the first to plug the lights in.

Their friend Pat Upton stopped by and asked, "Don't you want a T.V.?" The newlyweds smiled at each other and replied, "No, we don't need one." Almost two years without a television the newlyweds chased each other with giggles while the neighbors enjoyed the entertainment.

Web Pierce crooned in the background of their shiny new castle on wheels while Linda set a lovely dinner table for two. One night her husband returned home to their castle with sweaters tucked under his arm. The new bride asked her groom, "Where'd those come from?"

Without hesitation, John picked up a mug from the dinner placing, hurled it across the trailer and smashed it to smithereens. He shouted his diatribe with vehement language which when translated said, "Can't I have my own life?" The new bride ran into their tiny bedroom, throwing herself onto the bed as she wept. The groom followed and apologized for his outburst while he brushed tears from her eyes. He didn't know what came over him and promised to never do that again.

The honeymoon glow began to fade.

FIVE

The Pink House

1963 - 1967 (birth to four)
House #1 ~ Monroe

The couple, John and Linda, were about to give birth to their first child, me, so they purchased a tiny home on Hammertown Road. According to the historian, it had once been a two-room schoolhouse known as the Walkers Farm School House[4] in Monroe, Connecticut. It was at least 100 years old but the earliest attendance record they could find only dated back to 1912.

Walkers Farms 1912-1913

My parents purchased the school house two weeks before I was born in 1963. The price today would be considered a steal, but in their day ten thousand dollars was a lot of money. Because the home was pink, our family referred to it as the Pink House.

Settled into their second home, the devoted young wife desired to please her husband. She mentioned that she was going to cook him a roast for dinner.

"That sounds good, can you put cloves in it?"

"Sure if you'd like."

Excited, she prepared a classic pork roast dinner while he was at work. She rubbed the roast with cloves, salt and pepper and then made random slits with a knife to stuff with more cloves. Because that's what she had learned.

After a day's work, the young man came home to eat dinner with his wife. Within seconds, the first bite into the meal set a series of explosive events into motion. The universal mystery, 'Do Pigs Fly?' was answered. With the flick of John's wrist, the pork roast flew across their tiny kitchen, sailed over his wife's head, and landed on the floor with an unappetizing thud.

Startled and shocked at the sudden outburst Linda stammered, "What happened?"

John barked, "What are these damn things in here?"

"Cloves like you asked for." Tears streamed down her confused face. "I thought you'd be pleased?"

He shouted, "Garlic cloves, not whole spice cloves!"

Linda learned something new that day about her culinary skills and her Prince Charming.

When I turned one, my baby sister came along. Of course I don't remember her being born, but after four years at this house, some memories survive.

What family didn't have a one-piece blanket sleeper? Mine was pink and I'm sure it wasn't because we had a pink house. The contraption was like a giant fuzzy pillow case with a zipper up the front and sleeves for my arms.

Think sack races with burlap bags. I laughed trying not to slip and fall. Years later, it was passed on to my brother.

I had a favorite doll with blonde hair and blue eyes.

Because our home was tiny the coffee table was pushed against the living room wall to make room for the Christmas tree that blocked the front door. My sister and I giggled as we crawled under the table to hide in our new fort.

When Mom went back to work, she dropped me and my two-month-old sister off at our neighbors who babysat us on a regular basis. The Harrison girls who were a little older loved to carry my sister around because she was little and adorable. I liked Mr. Harrison because he comforted me when I was upset about something one day.

A couple of years into this routine, I decided to take a

walk down the road and headed straight to their house. My sister, who became known by me as my 'lil shadow, followed me on my first expedition. Mom recalled, "Mrs. Harrison took a switch to your legs all the way back home to ensure you'd never leave our yard again without an adult."

Another time when my sister and I wandered too close to the road, our family dog Schotzie bolted across the lawn and herded us back into the yard like we were sheep.

Mom had a few other people lined up to watch us when the Harrison's couldn't. One babysitter's house had a little hill where I sat alone on the lawn eating Cap'n Crunch with Berries out of the box. I remember being sad as I gazed out to the street waiting to be picked up.

Another babysitter's house had a tractor shaped mailbox, geese as tall as me that chased us kids around their yard and bees in the clover. As fast as I stepped on a bee I dropped to the ground and cried. The older boys, six and seven, ran to my rescue, picked me up and carried me inside so the babysitter could attend to my sting.

In June of 1967, my dad, thirty-two years old, was hospitalized because his appendix burst. The Bridgeport Sunday Post[5] had a full news article about his five-week hospital stay. Dad was a hemophiliac which meant his blood didn't clot. He was missing clotting factor VIII.

When the average person receives a cut, it begins clotting right away which slows down the bleeding until it stops. However, because hemophiliacs are missing the clotting factor they continue to bleed and could even bleed to death. Therefore, a burst appendix wasn't a good thing. The only reason he survived was that a refrigerated blood centrifuge machine had recently been purchased and installed with donated funds at St. Vincent's hospital in Bridgeport.

New Method Blood Record Set, In Massive Aid for Monroe Man

A Monroe man, who is a hemophiliac, has received his weight—normally about 135 pounds — in blood plasma, made possible by a relatively new method of blood donation at St. Vincent's hospital.

John G. Peterson, a 33-year-old house painter of 414 Hammertown road, Monroe, used the equivalent of approximately 125 pints of plasma—245 units—during his five week stay in the hospital for removal of an inflamed appendix.

The new method was available because of the recent installation of a refrigerated blood centrifuge at the hospital.

A Record Amount

According to the Connecticut Red Cross, Mr. Peterson used the largest amount of plasma ever recorded for a single case in the state, Dr. Robert Hentschel, the surgeon who operated, said.

Today Mr. Peterson, married and the father of two young daughters, expressed his gratitude for the massive effort employed by the hospital. He is recuperating at home.

Mr. Peterson, who entered St. Vincent's hospital early in June, was discharged in good condition during the second week in July after having received 245 units of fresh frozen plasma, much of it obtained by plasmapheresis, a relatively new method of blood donation made possible by the recent installation of a refrigerated blood centrifuge in the hospital's blood bank.

A First for Area

St. Vincent's is one of approximately six hospitals in the state to have such a centrifuge and the only one in the Bridgeport area.

The massive effort included utilizing donors from the Bridgeport chapter of the American Red Cross, doctors and other hospital personnel.

The hospital's blood bank staff, under the supervision of Miss Marguerite Cassidy, R.N., performed 19 single unit and 14 two unit plasmapheresis during Mr. Peterson's hospitalization. A unit equals 250 to 300 cubic centimeters—about a half a pint.

In addition, whole blood was taken from 79 standard donors and this whole blood was then centrifuged to obtain plasma. Additional supplies of frozen plasma were obtained from the Red Cross Blood center in Hartford.

"We would have been severely handicapped in supplying the patient the volume of fresh, frozen

(Continued on Page Three)

GRATEFUL FAMILY — John Peterson, a hemophiliac who has survived an appendectomy thanks to the availability of blood plasma, recuperates at home with the encouragement of his wife and daughters, Tammy Sue, three, and Cindy Jo, two. Mr. Peterson received 125 pints of plasma through a new method made possible by the recent installation of a refrigerated blood centrifuge at St. Vincent's hospital.

"According to the Red Cross, Mr. Peterson used the largest amount of plasma ever recorded for a single case in the state…"

My dad received 125 pints of plasma made possible with this new machine. According to the article, he received his weight in plasma, 125 pints to his 125 pounds.

While Dad spent five weeks in the hospital, we spent much time at Aunt Dee and Uncle Joe's. Mom witnessed her sister pray with thanksgiving at every meal so she brought that habit into our home. When Dad returned from the hospital he was happy to participate until my mother suggested he didn't sound serious enough when it was his turn to pray. He never said grace again.

The photo in the newspaper article shows a family celebrating. It didn't reveal our financial struggles, or that my sister and I started being dropped off at a variety of babysitter's homes throughout our preschool years when Mom decided to return to work.

Memory Mom shared: "When we lived in the pink house, the old two-room schoolhouse, you girls came out from your nap to say goodbye to your new friends Aunt Cookie and Uncle Rick who were visiting for the first time from New York City. Your father scolded you to go back to bed. I told him you girls just wanted to give hugs and say goodbye to your new friends. Your father said a few choice words to me in front of our guests. I was so upset that as soon as they left I got in the car and drove to my sister's and cried. After she consoled me I felt recharged. Encouraged and ready to go back home I assumed everything would be better. As soon as I pulled in, your father was waiting. 'Two can play that game.' He hopped in his truck and pulled out of our driveway threatening to never return. Running down the road I screamed for him to come back. I was scared and thought 'how could I be a single mom with two young toddlers.' Eventually he came home and we never talked about the matter again."

SIX

The Green House

1967 (age four)
House #2 ~ Newtown

Newtown, Connecticut was founded in 1705. Our first Newtown home was a temporary stop and a driveway's length from route 25. Startled by a long loud whistle, me and Shadow ran to the back yard in time to watch a train as it chugged its powerful engine down the RR tracks. Excited, we jumped and waved with glee and shouted, "choo choo, choo choo." Of course for the safety of our limbs a new rule was implemented; no going on the tracks, near the tracks or watching the train up close. All of them were off limits!

My sister and I came home from the Charlie Brown

Fair wearing colored construction paper hats, painted faces and each carried a gold fish in a plastic bag with water. With the RR backyard off limits, we were playing in front wearing our fair hats when a big car pulled up slow then stopped at the curb. In the 60s it wasn't uncommon for cars to be big, however the window rolled down and the man started talking to us so I walked towards the car. I don't know if divine intervention or mother intervention ruled the day but I hesitated and stopped.

Kids played and hovered around the dining room table with pop-up toys. We licked the bottom of the toy to help the suction stick to the table then pushed down with all our might on the variety of figures we each had. We waited to see whose pop-up toy would jump up first. Pop. Pop. Pop. Giggles and laughter erupted as the figures sprang one by one into action landing on the floor, falling on their side, whacking someone's head, or springing into the glass door of the kitty-corner cabinet. On cue we'd run out the front door, around the house, up the back stoop and we'd enter into the narrow kitchen running past the adults who smoked and played cribbage. Festivity was in the air. Everyone was having fun.

One evening my sister and I waited with Dad in the living room for our mom to return home from her church meeting. Dad sat on a chair facing the window while my sister and I shared his lap, close enough to touch the glass. We all peered into the dark and watched for Mom's headlights to pull into the driveway. My sister smiled while Dad balanced us on his knees. Perhaps family lore was woven into that serene moment, but there is no photo or journal to manipulate this image. The huge plate glass window holds the faintest memory of a brief moment of sweetness, proof that his affection was once there.

SEVEN

AUNT PARK LANE

1967 - 1971 (age four to seven)
House #3 ~ Newtown

*H*ow many four year olds can say they lived in three houses in one year?

Pulling into the driveway of our new home I peered out the window from the back seat of the car. Wow, look at that, as I played a solo I spy game. When the car stopped, I jumped onto the dirt driveway and ran to what caught my eye, a jungle of wild uncut grass. It isn't every day a four-year-old stands in a sea of grass almost as tall as her age, four-feet high.[6] It was magical, odd and exciting.

Once settled, we had a winter of deep snow. Bulky jackets with fuzzy trimmed hoods framed our frozen faces with red runny noses. Exposed wrists were raw and numb because the snow-coated mittens never covered that spot. Nevertheless, my sister and I had fun as we formed snow tunnels until we saw the light of the bluebird day. A freeze-frame moment so rare in the photo album of my mind whispered that Dad helped us dig our tunnel.

Nature can be enchanting and magical for a kid. When translucent silk threads hung from trees or floated in the air like festive strings absent of their balloons, the inchworms of spring were in abundance. Summer ushered in a bounty of butterflies which flit from flower to flower as they shared their calming melody.

Across the road was a swamp where we witnessed frequent turtle crossings. One day I fed a lanky piece of grass to a cute turtle who found his way into our yard. This slow creature lunged for the blade and clamped down on my thumb already bandaged from being slammed in a car door. I cried as the snapping turtle dangled from my sore thumb.

One day riding back from the grocery store with Mom I heard a rustling noise. Quiet. Rustle. Quiet. Rustle. I wondered where it was coming from. Was a ghost playing a game with me? "Aha," I shouted. It's the white bag sitting next to me on the bench seat of our car. I knew what jumping-beans were, but never heard of a noisy moving bag. Mom smiled, "Go ahead look." Somewhat afraid, I unfolded the top of the bag and peered inside. Not sure who startled who first but with a gasp I shrunk back at the movement of the claw and beady eyes staring at me. I had seen my first live lobster in a bag. Mom and I giggled.

Bordenko's Deli was located in Newtown Center. The deli had old uneven wooden floors that creaked and echoed with each step letting anyone know someone was in the store. During an errand with Mom, she shopped, paid the cashier and loaded my sister and me into the back seat of the car. About to pull out of the parking lot, she glanced in the rearview mirror and asked, "What's in yer mouth?" Proud of my acquisition and because I was busy chewing, I grabbed my sisters' wrist and held her hand up to expose the unopened piece of Bazooka bubble gum. Mom threw the car in park, shut it off, marched us back into the deli and made us apologize to the clerk for stealing one-cent gum. As if that wasn't enough, she made us pay two whole pennies for both pieces. Who knew those things at eye level weren't up for grabs? But Mom imparted a valuable life lesson on the four-year old that I was.

One afternoon, on the couch with Mom, she read me a story about a giraffe that swallowed a whistle. Trying to imagine what a giraffe felt like with a whistle stuck in his long spotted neck, I took a deep breath, inhaled, and sucked in through pursed lips. I surprised myself when I made a high-pitched whistle noise.

My favorite doll followed me from the pink house and then it went bye bye. I don't know where, but I was very sad. Four and heading off to kindergarten was a new experience for me. I wasn't confident I could entrust my toys to my three year old sister, Cindy Jo, so on my first day of school I left her and Mom with the most intelligent instructions a four-year-old could impart, "Don't let er play with my toys. Nothin' better be broken when I get home." Mom assured me they'd be safe in the closet. After school, I ran straight to the closet and discovered a broken toy. I was mad so I cried.

Memory Mom shared: *"After you girls went to school, I would go in your room and pick up all the toys and place them neatly in your toy box. Then I'd put the puzzles together and dress your dolls and put them in your toy box. When you girls came home, the toys you didn't care about when they were scattered over your room, suddenly became like new toys and you couldn't wait to play with them. They were soon scattered over your floor, but for a while you girls had a lot of fun. I thought you'd like to know, in case you don't remember this."*

Grammy and her second husband George visited for a few weeks on their way to Florida. They slept in their travel trailer which was parked in our driveway. Grumpy George would read the paper on our back porch lined with green wavy fiberglass. I never heard him utter a word until Sunday morning when I read the Beetle Bailey comics over his left shoulder. He snapped, turned and barked because he didn't appreciate the carrot I chewed in his ear. I was no longer interested in getting to know him. Even Grammy called him grumpy. Soon after, he retired to their trailer until they departed weeks later.

Eager to show Mom what I'd learned in school one day, I ran up the stairs of the back porch, past the Marcus Dairy milk box and entered into the kitchen. The door slammed behind me when I ran through the house beaming with excitement. "Mom! Mom! Where are you?" She followed me back to the kitchen where I held a piece of lined paper against the wall with my left hand and gripped the pencil with my right. Determined to be accurate, I formed one letter at a time until I spelled my first name and attached it to our family's last name. Thirteen letters later, I was proud to show Mom who I was.

Our rural neighborhood was on the outskirts of the Hattertown Historical District. We had a few neighbors and a handful of kids to play with. My sister at four, me at five, weren't allowed to play in the narrow streets. However, one day I took a risk and joined the kids. Par for the course, my sister,

also known as C.J., tagged along. No matter what I did, she was always my Irish twin shadow.

Well wouldn't ya know, coming down the road was Dad's company truck for Bambi Bread. Panic set in. Using youthful wisdom, C.J. followed me as we scrambled up the steep hillside just past our driveway and hid behind the rocks. Dad's truck, slow and decisive, continued down the road, past  our driveway and as if with magnetic force, stopped below the rock where we hid. He stepped out of the truck and used his parental rights as he demanded, "Get down from there now and get back into our yard!"

Stuck in our yard, the only other kids to play with were the boys next door. We called them the Hamburger brothers because we couldn't pronounce their last name. They were a little older than C.J. and me so what were we going to do with them? One day they buried batteries in our front yard and told us they were bombs. My sister and I screamed our way into the house. Mom's maternal advice was to go back outside and fight our own battles. We did. We plopped ourselves down on the front concrete stoop and waited. We didn't blow up. Chalk one up for Mom.

However, scaring us with their boyish pranks did not reflect the good spirit of their hearts. One day the older Hamburger brother saw me struggle to ride my bike so he brought his big-boy-ten-speed bike over to our driveway, leaned it against the stone wall and helped me climb on. The tip toes of my sneakers brushed the pedals. No training wheels were needed as he guarded and guided me along.

Me and C.J. shared a bedroom with windows conventional to ranch houses. Rather than tall windows that one walked up to and looked out, these were horizontally long and narrow and closer to the ceiling. During nap time I would lay on my bed, look up at the window and catch glimpses of butterflies flitting by.

Mom sometimes read bedtime prayers from the 1962 book <u>We Say Our Prayers</u>.[7] Apparently I started showing signs of my secretarial skillset at an early age because I'd numbered each prayer consecutively with a pencil and

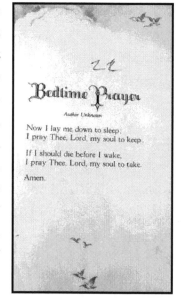

included my name and our home phone number. I wasn't sure what it meant to *die before I wake*, but the angels praying on the blue cover were the gate keeper of the prayers inside. To this day, a gorgeous majestic sunset with rolling clouds reminds me of a scene in this book. The image burned so strong that I dug up my book from the archives, determined to find the picture. Now in my fifties I smile because the image from my childhood that gave me comfort is more vivid in my mind than what exists in the book. Perhaps my imagination was working beautifully during a time of youthful innocence and childlike belief.

Maybe the image had been imprinted in my heart's mind as a beacon of hope and peace for my future.

One day after school, curiosity expanded my desire to explore unfamiliar territory; the swamp woods on the other side of our property's fence line. A place I wasn't supposed to be. Nor was my little shadow, who always followed. A few yards into this epic exploration, our house in full view, I tripped, fell backwards and landed on dead wood which punctured the back of my thigh. A jagged piece of wood jutted out of my leg. The pain I was in didn't compare to the immediate growing anxiety of him  finding out. I limped into the house with my sister. When I realized Dad wasn't home from work yet, I heaved a sigh of relief.

"Mom, mom, can you get this thing out of me?"

"Why are you crying? What happened?"

"I fell on a stick. See, it's stuck in me. It really hurts."

"Let's see honey. Wow that's a pretty good size chunk. Where were you?"

"The woods over there."

"I'm sorry but you're gonna to have ta wait till your father gets home. Sit there on the couch until he comes in."

Mom's response deflated me and now I was scared. By age five, the undercurrent of fear was palpable along with the tangible disconnect to my father. But my orders were to wait on the couch and so I waited for him to come home. It wasn't the painful gash in my leg that stung so much as the growing fears. I don't know who tended to me and wrapped my thigh with gauze, perhaps they both did when he returned home from work.

Let's face it, I should have felt some dread for having disobeyed my parents, but at the same time, relief knowing my daddy would be home soon to rescue me from this injury and eager to be saved and comforted by him. But that feeling never came.

Like the day we played in the street, I realize we were young so one could argue my dad expressed his paternal concern for our safety. However, when I reflect on the discipline I received in the early years, I recall a hard edge of anger rather than a stern chiding laced with love.

For the most part, I was obedient, but as children do, I tempted fate and bent parental rules. Consequences should breed wisdom. That is why parents are the parents. One of their jobs is to teach us along the way. But another one of their jobs is to love and protect their children. I believe a child should feel safe to come to their parents. Of course we screw up, test the waters and push the proverbial envelope. We're kids. I know there is no formula. No parenting manual. I know every home and upbringing remain different. Our emotions wax and wane. Our backgrounds, culture, race, religion, and experiences often shade our differences.

Navigating through the innocent childhood landmines filled with skinned knees, car doors, lobsters, battery bombs, bullies and whatever else came my way was hard enough.

However, when I encountered the sharper edge of consequences, a punishment that didn't seem to fit the crime, I began to sense a fear of a different kind. Because I was in kindergarten, I had no words to describe the uneasy sensation beginning to grow in me.

By age five I was already giving birth to a survival instinct which began to take root in me before I knew what it was, or what to call it.

> ...I began to sense a fear of a different kind.

No sooner had I put Ovaltine in my milk, the front legs of my chair raised off the floor as Dad lifted the other end of our kitchen table. The abrupt move tilted my chair backwards which forced me to grip the tables' chrome edge to keep from falling. My glass of chocolate milk slid and then tumbled over onto the floor. I was upset because I'd just stirred the chocolaty malt powder to perfection. Next, the Marcus Dairy glass milk bottle slid past me, over the edge and crashed on the floor. Chunky jagged pieces of milk glass, not the antique kind, lay near my chair now balanced on its two back legs. In milliseconds, our supper followed and then landed somewhere in the same vicinity of the broken bottle. To keep from falling backwards I continued to hold tight as my feet swung in their buster brown shoes, until Dad

> Don't let go,
> don't let go,
> hold on, hold on,
> keep holding on
> or you will fall!

composed himself and let the table back down.

Shattered glass reflected our supper and my Ovaltine. I wanted to cry, but a natural impulse suggested this wasn't one of those times.

From the kitchen where I had proclaimed with pride our family name, Dad commanded my mother, my sister, and me to, "Clean up the damn mess!" He then stormed out with a rage no one dared question. His problem was his mess. His mess was now our problem and it followed me into my adult years with a pursuit bent on depriving me of any peace or hope.

...a pursuit bent on depriving me of a peaceful hope.

EIGHT

Moving Day 1971

House #4 ~ Sandy Hook

I drove down Route 34 in Sandy Hook scanning the left lane until I found the entryway to Zoar Cemetery. The iron gate was open. I drove up the steep and narrow driveway to park, then walked along the old worn road searching for her headstone. It's never a straight shot but if I find the low steel-railing that guards another family plot, then I know I'm close. The old and tired cemetery has quietly held its post since 1767. I scanned the grounds until my eyes landed on the small weathered headstone. Nothing pretentious. Sandy's stone, simple and sweet, resembles the once pristine body that now lies underneath. A few engraved words mark my sister's fragile innocence. She is more precious than rubies; nothing you desire can compare with her. Proverbs 3:15 [9]

Sandra Gay Peterson
December 19, 1970
March 25, 1971

43

Carnation in hand, I paused for a moment. Like, what was I going to say to a slab of marble in an old plot of earth, grown over with the settling of time? How many people visit cemeteries and pour out their hearts like the person is sitting right there taking in every detail, while others look around nonchalant before giving a silent piece of themselves to something that already took a part of them away?

Bending at her headstone to have my moment, I glanced down the hill of the cemetery in time to see a Mayflower moving truck drive east on Route 34. I thought, *Hmmm, that's curious.* Turning back and giving her my full attention, I wondered what my sister would have been like had she stayed around. Would she have completed the part of our family life that seemed lifeless? Would she have been fun? Would we three sisters have been tight or aloof from one another? Would she and my brother be close? Would my brother have been born? When I'd exhausted my thoughts, I left the flower on the base of her headstone and prayed. Turning to leave, divine orchestration revealed another Mayflower truck only this time heading west.

In some odd way, I felt God was telling me, she was okay, I was okay and it was okay. Move on and let go.

March 25, 1971 was moving day. The Mayflower Moving Company showed up at Aunt Park Lane to pack up our home and move us to our new place on Route 34 in Sandy Hook.

The big long truck filled our driveway. Its colors were yellow and green and its logo donned the three-masted sailing ship of the Mayflower.

The privilege of carrying our three month old from the house to the car was mine. Attentive to the task, I calculated three cement steps down one at a time, careful not to trip or drop my baby sister. Conscientious, I held her delicate head in the crook of my left arm to keep her new neck from wobbling. From the steps, I continued along the sidewalk toward the car parked in the driveway. Almost there. One more step down. Phew! Safe! Relieved I didn't drop her, I placed Sandy into the car crib, a plaid rectangular bassinet that took up half the back seat. Having completed such a monumental task, an innate awareness of responsibility began. A sprout. A shift. A wave of duty. At that moment, the seven year old I was realized she was the oldest sibling.

Our fourth home was located across the street from the Sandy Hook volunteer fire substation with its yellow-blinking light. Sandy Hook was founded in 1711 and although considered a village in the town of Newtown, moving meant we would be transferred from Middle Gate School to Sandy Hook Elementary for the remainder of the year.

Mayflower movers began emptying their truck at the yellow house as they placed box after box into the living room. After some time, and with my new-found sense of responsibility, my thoughts turned to Sandy. I ran to the car anxious to check on her. On tiptoes, my hands and face pressed against the glass as I peered through the rear passenger window. I watched her baby blanket ebb and flow with each sleepy breath she took. Finally, in a fit of excitement, I ran to Mom, "Can I hold Sandy?"

"Wait 'til the movers set her crib up."

Now an impatient big sister, I ran back and forth to the car to check on her.

"Can I hold her now?"

"Wait 'till I tell you."

After what seemed an eternity, Mom announced, "The crib is ready, you can get your sister now."

Excited, I ran, opened the car door and leaned in. Careful to support Sandy's neck, I lifted her out of the car-crib and at the same time, grabbed her soft baby blanket. As I did, something seemed off. She looked different. She didn't look like she was sleeping anymore, but she didn't look awake. Something was wrong. She wasn't responding. Her neck didn't need the same support I'd given her that morning. She didn't feel like the same soft baby. She looked weird. Bluish-purple blotches colored her face and her fingers and toes.

Earlier, when I looked in on her she had moved. What changed? Cautious, I laid her back down with her blanket then ran for Mom. Back at the car, Mom gathered up her baby girl then erupted with hysterical cries. I didn't know the grave condition of Sandy but the somber air suggested something terrible happened. Mom sat in the driver's seat holding her baby chest to chest. Distraught, she accidentally banged Sandy's head on the steering wheel. Primal guttural cries welled up from her depths, "I'm sorry, I'm so sorry, I'm sorry, I'm so sorry." Rocking in rhythm to her sorrow, she cradled her baby as she apologized over and over and over for hitting her head.

Inconsolable, Mom continued to rock and comfort Sandy. Tears of disbelief streamed down her face hopeful they might water her little dead child back to life.

Mom's urgent tone demanded, "Get Cindy Jo, we have to leave now!" Unclear what happened, I stepped away from the car and walked the little sidewalk towards the house with a sense of duty to protect my

...she uttered primal guttural cries, "I'm so sorry..."

other sister, but from what, I didn't know. I was waiting for the crib to be set up. The air filled with distraught tension. Our new home still echoed from the emptiness of unpacked boxes and sparse furniture when I called out, "Cindy Jo, we have to leave." I thought I was calm, but she must have sensed concern because she burst out crying before we reached the car.

My mother cried. My sister cried. My father wasn't there. My baby sister was dead. I didn't cry. Instead I was mad. Mad she was dead. Mad I couldn't be her big sister anymore. And I was mad at my mother because she made me wait for the crib to be set up so I blurted, "She wouldn't be like this if I coulda held her when I asked." I replayed in my head each time I ran back and forth to the car and watched her blanket move with each breath. I waited to hold her. Waited to help. Waited to pick her up so I could carry her to her crib. I'd done such a good job when I carried her to the car. I didn't even drop her. And now she was dead.

Mom drove us to the hospital. Dad was somewhere in town finalizing the move. I later learned that people searched for him as the news was broadcasted throughout town over the CB scanner. They found him filling up at a local gas station on Church Hill Road where an attendant told him he needed to get to Danbury Hospital immediately.

When we arrived at the hospital, staff whisked my mother and Sandy away. That was the last time we saw the baby. Cindy Jo and I were turned over to a young pretty candy striper who wore a pink and white pinstriped smock. She ushered us to a backless wooden bench and tried making small talk to distract us from the event taking place. In an effort to fill the awkwardness of this uncomfortable moment, Ms. Candy Striper asked if we wanted to walk the halls of the hospital with her. "Yes," we chimed. It seemed like one big square as we walked straight down the hall from the entrance, hung a right and then another. Uneasiness from the days' event settled. I decided I didn't like the smell of hospitals. The girl was nice enough but I didn't like being there. This wasn't a fun moving day.

The halls did not look bright and cheery but rather dim in the aftermath. I knew Dad had arrived because as we approached where Mom had been waiting, his voice could be heard along with the inconsolable cries of my mother. We followed her wails to a door cracked open, but rather than rush into the room to see my parents, I hesitated and looked up at the candy striper for permission to enter. With her nod of approval, I poked my head in. With fire in his eyes, my father spit the words, 'Get the hell outta here!"

We didn't have a grave side service, rather her memorial was held at our church. I have no memory of attending nor does my mother recall if I was there. Following the memorial service people brought food to our empty home which was now tainted. As silhouettes mingled and whispered, the murmur of their conversations could be heard throughout the unfurnished rooms. I guess talking low showed respect for the dead, but she couldn't hear us anymore.

But life went on. Once all of our boxes were unpacked, I couldn't find my aluminum baton with white rubber tips. After the move it disappeared so I solicited C.J.'s services to help me find it. Leading the way, we searched every corner and closet in our new home but came up empty. Before going outside to check the yard I had a brainstorm.

"What if there's a hole in the floor of our closet and it fell through?"

"Let's look."

"That's kind of a hole don't ya think?"

"I dunno, maybe, sorta."

"Yah, I don't see how that could fit through. Ya know what, let's find the cellar and go look anyway."

We went into the dirty dug out basement and walked amid cobwebs but no luck.

"I dunno where else it could be. Maybe it fell out of a box on moving day. Let's go outside and check."

That's when we met our new neighbors, the Hall brothers. Ugh, boys, again.

Through the trees that bordered our property they shouted, "Whaddaya doing?"

We shouted back, "Trying to solve a mystery."

They invited us over to their yard but directed us to walk all the way back to the end of the tree line to get there.

"Why can't we cut through?"

"Because, um, well, there's an invisible electric fence between our yards."

We didn't believe them so we started to crossover.

"Stop," they shouted, "or you'll get zapped like bugs if you take another step."

We paused. They dared, "Don't believe us? Go for it." Well, after the battery incident with the Hamburger brothers we learned not to believe the boys. However, a little doubt decided we weren't ready to be fried like mosquitos. Reluctant, we walked to the end of the tree line and tried to look cool, not foolish.

After the welcoming initiation, we explained to the Hall brothers what we were doing. Without skipping a beat, they wanted to help find my baton and walked right through the middle of the invisible fence that wasn't there. My sister and I glared. Argghh, duped again!

But the innocence of uncalculating youthfulness has a resiliency which bounces back with unspoken forgiveness

and mercy, moving our playful steps forward to the next thing put on our path. We were quick to form the second grader detective team as our new friends joined the search. We never did find my baton. No one could explain how it disappeared. As any second grader could, I shrugged it off as an unfortunate loss and casualty of another move.

Moving meant my sister and I switched schools mid-year. Sandy Hook Elementary School was filled with strange faces except for two, our cousins, Nancy and Bobby. I was assigned to a desk which was shared with a new classmate. When I asked my classmate a question the second grade teacher walked by and with a stern face, whacked my knuckles hard with her ruler. The sting of her teaching method encouraged the numbing that was settling into my sad heart. I wasn't sure how I landed in this place, where my other friends were, or where my dead sister was, but with certainty I didn't like this crabby person with the ruler.

On the last day of school, the playground chatter took on a different rhythm while kids milled around the picnic tables, swung on swings, went up and down on seesaws, or spun round and round with dizzy glee on the metal carousel. Some took turns rocking back and forth on seated mechanical farm animals mounted on tight springs. Other kids sat on the cement wall swinging their legs. But we all sang to the lyrics being squeezed through the courtyard speakers. The melody of "Joy to the World"[8] sounded warped like a melted vinyl record wobbling around the turntable with a bullfrog sitting on it.

A few months into our home, I was curious one night to see what was behind a door in our living room. When I touched the door it felt so hot I thought there was a fire on the other side, but it was only the heat of summer beginning. When I opened it, I discovered a walk-up attic with a curious glow. Up the stairs I was drawn to a window ablazed and throbbing with orange and yellow. Mesmerized, I stared out at the fire house across the street. During the darkest part of night, the silent rhythm of the fire company's yellow-blinking light absorbed me into its pulse with an eerie glow. I stood quiet for the longest time.

In the whirlwind of the move, new school, teachers and classmates, someone forgot that this seven year old found her baby sister dead.

"Get the hell outta here," still rang in my ears.

NINE

The Day My Music Died

1971 - 1973 (age eight and nine)
House #5 ~ Newtown

A few months after Sandy died and second grade was over, my family moved back to Newtown to a brand new home Dad built on Washbrook Road. This had become his trade. This was the first new home I lived in.

The brown two-story colonial came with modern amenities; central vacuuming, dishwasher, fireplace, porches, four bedrooms, three baths and a full finished basement. The two car garage was bigger than our first home, the pink converted two-room school house. What ample space for our growing family whose baby boy would soon join us in December of 1972. As if waving us into the home stretch, this new luxurious house offered our family a fresh start for new beginnings.

Third grade and my own bedroom, I was excited to have a closet just for toys. The first order of business was to setup toy shop to situate my pink baton with green neon tips. This replaced the one that disappeared from the last move. The mystery of its whereabouts alerted me to pay extra attention to what wall I leaned it against before I went to bed. There'd be no uncertainty this time. Satisfied, I fell asleep. When I awoke in the morning it was gone. I couldn't believe it. Was I dreaming? I began to question if I really owned one.

Again, no one in my family had any idea where it was. Because I was sure they wouldn't lie and the only other person in my room was a Bobby Sherman poster, I assumed the obvious, I was robbed. Wearing my imaginary Sherlock Holmes hat, I searched the brand new shellacked floors for muddy footprints but no sign of an intruder. Determined to solve the mystery, I went outside and looked for clues.

I walked around the house looking for ladder marks in the grass. Although my juvenile sleuthing skills found no evidence, I concluded: in the middle of the night, a thief leaned a ladder against the house, climbed to my window, crawled through and continued like a snake on his belly. He swiped my baton and climbed back down the ladder lit by the glow of the neon tips. I couldn't explain the absence of ladder marks but how else could one explain the unexplainable?

Yet this time something new was born inside of me, something which weakened my confidence. Doubt. I questioned the certainty of what I thought I knew.

> ...something new was born inside of me...doubt.

As our lot in life would have it, once again my sister and I had new neighbors. Guess what they were? Boys. The Mackenzie boys. Not that there was anything wrong with them, but they were boys. Our reference thus far had been battery bombs and an invisible electric fence. Once settled into our new neighborhood, it didn't take long to wear a path between the two-acre back yards. However, a bit of trepidation lingered for we still hadn't received our welcome-to-the-neighborhood initiation.

Winter ushered in the welcoming committee during a snowball fight when my sister and I discovered the difference between snowballs, ice balls and snowballs with rocks. Regardless of the hard numbing stings that met our cold cheeks or other body parts, we pummeled snow and ice balls back at the fast and furious onslaught that tried to defeat us. Determined not to run away in tears, we claimed our spot behind our mighty two-foot high snow fortress. When it was all over, we cheered our victory.

Laura Sovereign, our paternal grandmother, came bearing gifts for my sister and me. We were meeting her for the first time that I recalled. History reported that she and my dad didn't get along very well. Like when his appendix burst, he didn't want his mother anywhere near the hospital. But on this particular day, she brought us toys; dolls about three feet tall and a pair of crutches. I'd never seen a doll as tall as me, so lifelike and amazing. I thought that was the coolest thing. Now the crutches, they were the next coolest thing. They weren't the same as stilts. I had a blast figuring out how to walk and swing my legs without falling. That was, until Dad yelled and put a cease and desist order on the crutches. He was enraged.

"Where'd those come from?"

"Gramma gave em to us to play with."

"Get the hell off of em. They're not toys. I never wanna see you on those damn things again."

Soon after meeting our grandmother, the dolls disappeared and the crutches were off limits. The word was she visited a few more times and always came bearing gifts but I have no recollection of ever seeing her again. Dad walked with a limp from a childhood knee injury he'd received when he was five. Because of his hemophilia it never healed properly. Perhaps the crutches his mother brought were from his childhood.

For Halloween, my sister and I set out into the cold October night walking down the steep driveway in mom-made costumes. Disguised as ghosts, sheets covered our heads and exposed our sneakers and pails. My nose was runny as I breathed in the night air through the sheet which clung to my mouth. Every few steps my costume slid on my head making it hard to see. Trying to realign the uneven holes with my eyes was a chore. If I pulled too far, my nose poked through the other eye hole.

When our elementary school held a Halloween party, Mom put together a princess dress with a homemade pointed hat adorned with flowing material. I walked down the dirt road to Middle Gate wearing my costume. Every step I took seemed to off center this round cone, making it lopsided on my head. No matter how many bobby pins Mom put in my hair, they wouldn't hold this crown in place as I brushed hair  and flowing material out of my face. In an effort to keep it from falling off, I tilted my head right to left as if I were a bobblehead princess. But by the time I arrived at school I was worn out from fighting the cone. Cap now in hand, I joined in tow with the other Halloween misfits gathering for the charade, I mean, parade. I'm not sure who invented Halloween but it's a lot of work for a little kid.

Aunt Dee, my mother's sister, and Uncle Joe arrived with their kids for a family reunion with our New York relatives. Our parents reintroduced us to Aunt Cookie and Uncle Rick, along with their three daughters, our cousins. Although I'd met Aunt Cookie and Uncle Rick at the pink house this was like the first real time for me because I was older.

Aunt Cookie, who is black, was a Fresh Air Child when she was six. In those days the Fresh Air Program[11] gave inner-city children an opportunity to experience a rural setting. Cookie, who lived in the Bronx, was sent to Springfield, Vermont in the 1940s to stay at Mom and Aunt Dee's childhood home. When my grandmother Ivis picked her up at the train station, she asked if she had a nickname she liked to be called. Constance proclaimed, "Cookie!" Mom was five, Cookie six and Dee was seven. From that summer on, began a friendship and kinship that never ended, only bloomed for the three sisters to this day.[12]

So in 1971 I knew nothing other than I was meeting my New York City relatives.

Mom told Cookie, "I prepared my girls to meet the black kids from the city." Cookie told Mom, "Well, I prepared my girls to meet the white kids in the country." They both had a good laugh over that one. Once they arrived, I didn't notice they were black any more than they noticed we were white. We weren't stupid. Of course we could see we each had different color skin and our hair looked different, but we didn't care, we just wanted to play and have fun. So we did. It was that simple.

Dad's surrogate parents were Jack and Irene. Irene was Hungarian and everyone called her Shorty, because she was, short that is. They acted as our grandparents because Dad had rented a room from them in his early twenties so by the time he and Mom met they had absorbed him into their family as if he was their own son. Therefore, we went to many of their family gatherings. Picnics consisted of macaroni salad, potato salad, deviled eggs, all were drowned in mayonnaise. I hate mayonnaise. The other specialty we were introduced to was jellied pickled pigs feet with black peppercorns sealed in the fat. Dad loved them therefore I learned to like them. For the holidays, Jack and Irene gave each of us kids a hollow chocolate Santa or hollow chocolate bunnies along with 50 cents. No matter where we sat in their home, we were sure to walk away with cat hair clinging to our clothes. We'd go to their summer lake house in the middle of the woods when the canopy of trees blocked the sun and the abundance of bugs made it not fun. To add to the excitement, the adults played cards, got drunk and yelled at who knows what. I never enjoyed going.

Hide and seek challenges one to find the most creative spot to, well, hide. Being the oldest and no doubt the smartest, Houdini juices flowed when I spotted the ultimate hiding place in the garage. Thinking I was rather clever I pulled up on the silver latch, lifted the lid of the big white freezer, hoisted myself up and stepped into the deep chest then lowered the lid. I crouched for a few minutes savoring my hiding spot until I was ready to get out. When I pushed the lid it clicked. This can't be good. The movement to free myself firmly secured the latch, locking out heat, light and oxygen and locking me in with cold stale air and frozen food. This was a stupid idea. I mean, it seemed like a good one at first. In a squatted position, I felt the four walls. Although dark, I looked up, sideways, and around. Not much room to do anything. The silence was dense. It had never occurred to me that at some point I wouldn't be able to breathe. Although dark, cold and somewhat anxious, I don't recall that I screamed or banged. Instead a calm panic started to set in. Whose dumb idea was it to play hide and seek anyway? Probably mine.

Voices could be heard and then the lid opened. Thank God Mom and my sister found me. I was cold and shook up and happy to get out of the freezer, until I faced the brown hollow door. I feared what retribution I'd get from Dad who sat on the other side of the door. As I followed Mom back into the house, I hesitated because my nervous stomach was doing flip flops, but nothing happened. I was met with annoyance, as if that was stupid. But nothing happened.

No warmth. No hugs. No kisses. No one fussed over me and wondered if I was okay. Nothing happened.

But nothing happened.

Cigarette ashtrays were part of the furniture in many households. These offensive ornaments could be on wooden stands positioned near the couch or recliner chair. Sometimes these big dark amber monstrosities adorned the center of coffee tables or other corners of a room. The brown glass indented on each side could be filled with ashes and remnants of unfinished cigarettes, some with shades of lipstick. Wherever they were, they were filled with filth. People smoked in homes, airplanes, work places, in the car with the windows rolled up, or at the laundromat while cleaning clothes. It wasn't uncommon to find cigarette butts stomped out on the floors of many public places even in the grocery stores. The list goes on.

Lucky Strike was Dad's brand of unfiltered poison every day of his adult life. One day my sister and I showed a curiosity about his daily habit. Dad said, "You want to know, I'll show you," and demanded we sit at the kitchen table while he handed each of us a cigarette. His thumb flipped open the lid of his silver lighter and one by one he lit them as our feet dangled above the kitchen floor.

I giggled as we awaited further instructions.

Dad exclaimed, "You will smoke the whole thing until it's gone."

But without a twinkle in his eyes, he further stated, "And you will inhale and hold the smoke in your mouths before exhaling!"

This wasn't at all what my sister and I had in mind when we asked Dad about his habit. As quick as the game began, it lost all appeal. It was no longer fun. We were no longer curious, but we could no longer walk away.

As we inhaled our first cigarette into our young lungs, we felt sick within seconds. I became lightheaded, green and woozy. My sister ran to the bathroom and threw up. My throw up never came out, so I was sick from head to toe. Nonetheless, I still had my orders to help clean up after supper. Sick as a dog I stood on a step stool at the sink and washed the dishes. Instead of putting an end to this cruel session, Mom stood on the sidelines doing nothing.

Perhaps this ridiculous exercise was laced with love in hopes we'd hate the taste and never smoke. I'm not convinced this tactic worked. My sister smoked. I didn't. We were little girls asking our daddy a question about something we witnessed him do. I learned inquiring minds do not want to know. More often than I cared for, "Do as I say, not as I do," was a common mantra in our home. Whatever the intention, it whittled away at my youthfulness as I learned in our home, curiosity kills curiosity.

> ...curiosity kills curiosity.

Guests milled throughout our house one Christmas as aunts, uncles and cousins celebrated in our new home. My sister and I received red dresses. A couple "ooohs," and "ahhhs," insisted we try them on so some relative could capture the gift in a photo.

Dressed for display, I walked back into the kitchen where people mingled and leaned against the counter. Dad laughed, "That dress makes you look fat." Two of my boy cousins mimicked their Uncle John's laugh and repeated, "You look fat." I froze and wished I hadn't put the stupid dress on, but I was following orders. I was embarrassed and I was sure everyone had heard.

That Christmas moment was forever recorded on film. The photo reminds me I was humiliated by my dad and in front of guests. It revealed how one click can capture the fragile and fractured heart of a little girl desperate for her father's admiration. An unexpected word, now silent in the photo, reminds me how I started to become fat and ugly through my lens of myself. The Polaroid that never fades reminds me why I never felt pretty, especially in Dad's eyes.

> The Polaroid that never fades....

The only camping I did with my family was from under the blanket tent I helped to put together in C.J.'s bedroom. We slung blankets over chairs and tucked corners inside of dresser drawers to hold them in place. Once camp was set up we grabbed the radio and sat inside our tent.

The 1960s ivory colored box had magic in the plastic knobs which were painted with lines and numbers. I'd turn the knob back and forth in search of a radio station that played music. Hissing sounds mixed with faint melodies told me I was about to capture a song behind the painted line so I'd hold my breath, as if that would help the station come in clearer. With finesse, I turned the grooved radio knob back and forth until I heard it catch the music. Once caught, it felt like an imaginary notch holding the station in place. Faint at first then like magic, it would become loud and louder until the hiss faded into the background and the song played robust and clear. Satisfied to have found the sweet spot, I could stop holding my breath and start singing.

One song in particular grabbed my attention. It went on and on as it told a long story about iconic musicians who had died. I didn't understand the lyrics, but I was swept away with the rhythm and sang along to the catchy chorus in "American Pie."[10] The depth of the song resonated in an unspoken way with the childhood music that was beginning to die in my soul.

Every day when my sister and I walked home from Middle Gate Elementary, we couldn't help but pass Lisa's house and the scene of the crime, her barn. One weekend when we had played with Lisa I slipped on hay and fell through the hole of the second floor and broke my wrist. By the grace of God I didn't hit the tractor engines which formed a circle below.

So anyway, on this day walking home from school C.J. announced she had to go to the bathroom. "Oh?" I said.

Having been told to go straight home and make no stops posed a dilemma. Being the oldest, I took charge and calculated our options. To win or lose the game of the day depended on how I moved my pawn in the chess game. I was learning to anticipate every move before making a decision. If we stopped to use Lisa's bathroom, we risked getting in trouble. Go straight home? We risked wetting our pants. Come home with wet pants? We risked being put over Dad's lap to receive bare bottom beatings with his hands or belt. This had become standard operating procedure. Somehow, it was supposed to stop us from wetting our pants.

After what felt like an hour of contemplating the dreadful consequences, my elementary logic came up with the easiest and safest choice. I decided we should go to Lisa's house so my sister could avoid the repercussion of going home with wet pants. My decision meant we were disobeying the after school rules that said, make no stops. Anxious, we ran and knocked on the door. It felt like forever but then the door opened. I paced back and forth in their cluttered narrow hallway, waiting for C.J. to finish her business. Agitated I wondered what took her so long, but it was probably only a minute. Then all of a sudden I had to pee. For a split second I thought, *hold it until you get home, we have to get out of here.* But I decided I didn't want to get beaten with his belt this time either, so I peed as fast as I could. With fear and urgency pulsing through my veins, we left abruptly. Satisfied that we were delivered from what could have been a calamity we breathed a sigh of relief. "Phew, close call."

Back on the dirt road heading home, C.J. showed a curiosity about the board game I carried so we stopped and squatted in the middle of the road to show her the game then continued home.

As soon as we walked through the front door, his voice beckoned, "Tammy Sue, get in here now." Guess Dad was home early. I snapped to attention, but moved ever so slow. I followed the voice down the hall and found it sitting in the vinyl cushioned chair at the kitchen table. Mother stood behind the chair where the voice sat.

When I entered the kitchen, I stopped, stood and froze. A few feet away, with his eyes of steel he called, "Get over here." My legs became cement, but I managed a few more steps until I found myself standing between his knees.

Being the oldest had its downside for sure. Usually I was the one who met the inquisitions.

"Where were you, why were you late?"

"We stopped in the road to look at the board game I was carrying."

SMACK! Right across my face went his big calloused hand as he called me a liar.

"I'll ask you again, where were you? The truth, capiche?"

My answer remained the same.

His response remained the same. SMACK!

My nose was now bleeding.

I hoped for Mom to do something in my defense.

Still in my school clothes, a white shirt with ruffles, plaid skirt, knee-high socks exposing knobby knees; the inquisition continued as he smacked my face, one firm blow after another. My nose continued to bleed with each swing of his hand. Blood dripped onto my white shirt while tears streamed down my stinging face. Never satisfied with my answer he continued to call me a liar as he smacked me into submission. Mom stood still, saying and doing nothing while her silence spoke volumes.

I grew numb.

I didn't know what else to say.

I didn't know what answer he wanted.

I didn't know what answer he would accept.

With discernment, I had gone into survival mode to protect my sister and myself from the other possible fate; the buckle of his belt which could have greeted our bare bottoms at the end of the day.

The vocal and silent messages I'd already received suggested there was no room for expression or conversation. In addition, his one-sided back-handed dialogues solidified for me that I didn't know how to make smart choices and clearly it wasn't safe to tell the detailed truth. His final blow confirmed that this wasn't my dad. At that moment, I was staring into the face of my enemy. For self-preservation, a switch in me turned off and I began to check out.

I was dismissed, grounded and sent to my room. I opened my bedroom window, masked my tears with a smile and shouted to the Mackenzie boy below, "I can't come out and play today."

> A switch in me turned off.

For some reason Mom seemed quiet and unruffled during Dad's tirades. Her manner had a way of making me think I deserved what I got. If I questioned an altercation, there were times she implied or so much as said, "You must've done something to make your father mad."

Then there were the other times when Mom found her voice when Dad wasn't around. Should we talk back in any manner, her finger and thumb snapped our lips before we could blink. She was the fastest lip-snapper on the east coast. Boy that stung. Mom translated the word geez as taking the Lord's name in vain so that guaranteed a mouth wash of Irish Spring soap.

In exasperation to anything that seemed to frustrate her, she chased my sister and me around our beds with the wooden spoon. The few times she missed and whacked herself harder than us, we laughed as soon as she left the room. But really none of this was funny. Instead, what hurt and confused me was Mom's need to defend Dad rather than defend us from the monster.

I felt alienated from my family, like I was the odd one out. It felt as if my mother liked my sister more than me. She was thin and cute and unlike me, she liked to cuddle on Mom's lap. She even looked related to Mom, both with their fine long brown hair. In fact, my brother had blonde hair and my Dad's was black. I came out with red hair. Maybe that was why I never felt connected. Mom often joked that our milkman had red hair and she'd laugh, "And besides I was asleep when you were born." She meant no harm. It was supposed to be funny, but I had hoped there was truth in her wry humor because it would explain the separation I felt.

Through this day to day existence I appeared normal, but indifference began to settle into my soul that was being chipped away so I built a new wall around me and detached. I started shutting down as the spirit of life and the music inside of me dissolved, not overnight, but a little at a time, until they died.

Indifference began to settle...

The air of our brand new home became permeated with anger, tension, and fear. Anxiety and trepidation stirred with each move I made.

Yet life went on. For roughly two years I lived in this home. Our dog was Duke. Princess the Siamese cat hid her kittens inside the bathroom wall. I fell in love with Donny Osmond and Bobby Sherman. I wore out my Alfred Hitchcock album of Ghost Stories. C.J. and I sat on our parent's bed and watched the Wizard of Oz on an eight-inch black and white television. During a commercial break, Mom explained that a baby was in her huge belly. Grandmother stayed for a spell to help Mom after our brother was born. I babysat the classroom pet mouse. Grandmother hated mice. Holidays were spent with tradition and we went to church without Dad.

"I like you a lot.
I know that you like gum.
Here is ten pennies for
some gum."

TEN

A Bowl of Onions

1971 - 1973 (age eight and nine)
House #5 ~ Washbrook Road, Newtown

The kitchen table commander shouts, "Finish eating or else!" I prompt myself to remember the code; keep your head down and avoid eye contact.

"Eat everything on your plate, there are starving kids in China."
"I work hard to put a roof over your head and food on the table."
"If you don't eat your food in the next five minutes, you'll get more."

If I'm lucky, I'll get through supper without my parents' chastising glare. But when they decide to wait for me to clean off my plate, the timer gets set. The race is on. The air is thick as I face off with the plate of food I already hate. The longer I stare at it, the colder it gets, making it taste more vile then when we first sat down to eat. Hastily I try choking down the cold and unwanted food, but at this stage, nothing can make it taste good or slide down easy because the tension is shutting down all my internal systems. I cannot cry because it won't help. Nobody will care. And should I cry, they will give me something to cry about.

Many suppers had been thrown on the floor and across the room. I guess those meals were different. They must have known starving kids from China wouldn't eat that food.

Second helpings of the main course waited for me in case I didn't finish the first. Dessert followed every meal. A cake of sorts and the store brand ice cream stocked the freezer.

During a typical meal the wooden salad bowl was filled with iceberg lettuce, onions, cucumbers and tomatoes. I was creative in how I navigated through the explosion of onions, making sure to avoid those smelly white chunks that made my eyes sting and water. Satisfied with my selection, I continued eating. When supper was over, Mom and C.J. rose and cleared their plates from the table so I stood and excused myself to join them. As if on cue, Dad said, "Sit back down." With an even set jaw and stern tone he stated, "Now finish eating what's left in the salad bowl." I looked at the bowl then back at him, but he wasn't kidding.

I sat in my chair, turned away from Dad and faced the salad bowl. I reached my arms up and into what seemed like a bottomless pit of onions. While he glared from the head of the table, I ate one onion after another while stifling back tears and onion stings. I was made to eat all the onion chunks that had found their way to the bottom of the bowl. The same onions the rest of the family had dodged.

I never received my father's love or approval in a way that would make me believe I was pretty, loved or even wanted. What little girl should not want that from her daddy?

And I knew I wasn't his Princess because ... Princesses are not forced to eat a bowl of onions.

> ...Princesses are not
> forced to eat a bowl of onions.

ELEVEN

I Could Fly

Mom always said I was the apple of his eye
Yet only storm clouds brewed in Daddy's angry eyes
Hopscotch memories washed away with rain
Hula Hoops and jump rope faded just the same
But I could fly
Fly far from the lie
With children's fearless wings
Where little ones are heard
Where prayerful angels sing
From the pain
I could fly[13]

TWELVE

Play it by Ear

The music in our home was broken. I don't know if we were out of tune or if life was out of tune. Maybe the record player was broken but it seemed either parts were skipped over or the same song kept being played. My dad, who was half Italian, called me stunod when I did something he thought was stupid, but maybe he was using the word wrong because stunod derives from stonato which means *out of tune.*

My grandfather, Robert Gay, a self-taught musician, played the fiddle. Dad, also a self-taught musician, played acoustic and electric guitar and learned the banjo. To help prepare for jam sessions, Mom pulled out her black manual typewriter to replicate song sheets of entertainers such as Hank Williams, Ray Price, Johnny Cash, Jim Reeves, Charlie Walker, Loretta Lynn and Webb Pierce.

Grandpa gave me one of his violins so I could begin lessons during fourth grade. Nestled inside the old black

74

tattered case was a horse-hair bow, pitch pipe, rubber band and sponge for my chin. Broken rosin sprinkled amber glitter throughout the dingy dark blue velvet lining.

After school I placed my beginner violin record on the turntable and practiced various techniques of Twinkle Twinkle Little Star. Much like Dad and Grandpa, I discovered a natural ability to play by ear. I was so excited when I made the connection from sound to ear to strings  without reading notes that I couldn't wait to show my teacher at school the next day. However, my fourth grade teacher wasn't impressed. She didn't seem to recognize the youthful enthusiasm that bubbled up in me. She never smiled. Instead she scolded me for playing my homework by ear and scolded me in front of my classmates. Embarrassed, I blushed and my smile melted away.

THIRTEEN

The Lake House

1973 - 1974 (age ten)
House #6 ~ Sandy Hook

"Let's hurry or we'll miss them," my sister and I said in stereo.

The electric can opener couldn't turn fast enough. Eager, we watched the blade cut tiny jagged teeth around the edge of the tin can. With slow awkward robotic movements, then a final ping, the magnet on the opener held the lid which released the canned corn to drop into my hands, splashing sweet liquid onto my fingers.

"Ready?"

"Ready!" We exclaimed with gleeful excitement.

Running out the back door, down the steps, the screen door slammed behind us. In rhythmic motion, it slowed down with each squeaky dense thud against the door frame until it fell silent. Holding the can upright, we sprinted across the back yard, past the tire swing, through the metal gate and down to the dock.

We took turns as we threw corn into Lake Zoar. One by one golden drops were illuminated by sun rays before they sank slowly out of sight into the murky water.

Casting our fishing lines, we'd wait. Bubbles appeared. Movement. Action. A corn kernel fiesta came to life with the frenzy of the fish feeding. "Did you see that?" "Look, more are coming!" "Oooh look how big that one is!" Most times, we only snagged catfish, but we didn't care. It was exciting to see the results of baiting a hook with a worm or corn tossed into the water. It was an innocent catch and release program.

Diving off the dock came with a price. We dared each other to jump in, touch bottom, grab anything, but don't you dare come back up empty handed. We'd shout, "I dare you to dive to the bottom with your eyes wide open." How could we prove it? We simply believed each other. Rising to the top all bubbles and giggles, we reported that we saw the bottom, or not, touched slimy seaweed, saw a rock or bass. We were excited to share about anything we saw under water, even if it was our hand inches from our face.

My sister and I were back to sharing a bedroom almost the size of a large walk-in closet so when the wicked thunder and lightning storm drove the rain sideways across the lake, I shot up in bed and almost whacked my head on the low sloped ceiling. One too many thunder booms later, C.J. and I decided we'd had enough so we burst into our parents' room, but their unwelcoming tones and growls commanded we go back to bed. Unsettled by the noise over the lake we were too shaken to fall asleep. Rather than count sheep we'd count the seconds in between thunder booms and lightning flashes until we were convinced that the lake storm had moved far away.

One day Dad took C.J. and me to one of his job sites. I sat sandwiched on the bench seat of his pickup truck while my feet straddled the hump. His eight-track played Charlie Pride's Mansion on a Hill. Sitting inside the cab of Dad's work truck wasn't commonplace so I felt like a visitor rather than his daughter. Even though I was wary, it was as if someone had left a door cracked open to his private room where I gained a glimpse of my dad's world. Dad talked with other construction workers about the house they would be renovating while we walked around junk piles and stepped on two-by-four sidewalks strewn on the lawn. Dad let us rummage through the things left behind from the previous owners with an understanding that we could keep what we found. My treasure was paper and a pocket folder. The variety of paper excited me; lined graph and tracing paper, and colored pink, green and yellow. This little find pumped my creative juices as I thought of the Sunday cartoons I might draw and what blueprints I might conjure up of my future home. I tucked them into the folder for safe keeping.

In fifth grade I started my second year of violin lessons. When I walked through the lake community of Shady Rest to the bus stop I'd pass Lucy's house up on the hill. She was a fifth grader from the neighborhood who had a horse named Candy that she wanted to sell. Lucy seemed mature and like her life was together because she owned a horse so I showed an interest in buying Candy. She wrote out her advertisement for me to take home and show my parents. It read:

Horse for Sale _a young Bay mare named candy. Good with children. 14 hands high. Color is Brown. Rides western or english. NO tack to Be Sold with her. For information call 426-3876 ask for edie call after 4:00 on weekdays. on weekends call anytime. 400.00 [sic]_

For safe keeping I tucked it under the extra set of strings in the violin case. I knew better than to ask my parents if they'd buy me a horse, but that didn't stop me from pausing at the crest of the hill every day on my way home from school. I gripped Grampa's violin case while I stared at her house and tried to imagine life with a horse named Candy. I resolved that the palomino model in my toy chest would have to do.

Over time the whimsical youthful dream faded. I'm not sure why I kept Lucy's note tucked in my violin case these many years later, unless, it was to remind me of me; a young girl who dreamed and imagined something.

My brother Michael was just a few months old when we moved to the lake house. He is nine years my junior and because I helped Mom a lot, he was my first babysitting job. To keep him from becoming pigeon-toed, I exercised his feet by turning them out and in, out and in, out and in while he lay on the white wicker changing-table.

Michael also came with a baby bottom and a diaper which had to be changed regularly. As he lay on the table, my left hand would hold his feet up in order to clean his little butt. Once diaper rash ointment and baby powder were applied, I laid a cloth diaper under him. Folding and fastening the diaper with baby colored safety pins took focus, strength and strategy. He could laugh, cry, squirm, contort, kick his legs, or pee while I tried to stick the pin through the folded corners, keep it taut, and at the same time try not to stab either of us. Pinned and with no injuries to speak of, I'd slip plastic pull-up-pants over his fresh diaper. To complete the task at hand, his dirty cotton diaper had to get dunked in the toilet before going into the hamper.

Having a baby brother prepared me for my first *paid* babysitting job. The next door mother solicited my fifth grade services so she could run a quick errand in town. She greeted me at the side door and welcomed me in. I was both excited and apprehensive but she seemed confident that I could manage the task. My job was to sit on her couch in case her baby woke from his nap. Should that have happened I imagine I was instructed to call my Mom who was at home. Although I never heard him cry, I checked on him several times during the two hours his mother was gone. When she returned she was pleased to find everything okay. Before leaving she invited me to sit and visit with her at her little kitchen table. When she shared what she was making for dinner I must have scrunched my nose because she engaged me in a conversation about what foods I disliked. "Well, I'm not crazy about mushrooms or peppers, but I'm willing to try mushrooms again."

"What about onions?"

Without reservation, "I especially hate onions."

Before going home to dinner she paid me 50 cents for the two hours I was there and asked if I'd be willing to watch her son another time. Of course I said yes. She made sure I knew that evening rates were 50 cents an hour.

We grew up eating Wonder bread, baloney, yellow mustard, and fluffernutter sandwiches, iceberg lettuce, overcooked meat, Friday fish sticks and canned vegetables. Our scrambled eggs were stretched with bread and milk. To this day I don't know why canned vegetables were boiled to death. I hated canned asparagus; the slimy green weed was putrid. Okay, now the mayonnaise jar, forget it, I wouldn't touch it with a ten-foot pole. Mom introduced us to some of her favorites, iceberg lettuce sprinkled with sugar, and spaghetti floating in milk sprinkled with salt and pepper. Cake-pan-cake which was a chocolate cake made in the pan, and lemon meringue pie with loads of stiff beaten egg whites piled on top. She didn't care for much sauce, mushrooms, fish or anything spicy.

Dad on the other hand liked hot sauce, spices and seafood such as stuffed clams, long-neck steamers, raw clams and oysters on the half-shell, escargot and linguine piled with seafood floating in red sauce. A bottle of Tabasco sauce and Worcestershire sauce could be found in our fridge. Besides Schaefer or Budweiser beer, he always had a cup of hot Lipton tea.

One afternoon I had the kitchen all to myself while my family was in the backyard. Armed with the necessary tools to make a cake; stainless steel mixing bowl, electric hand mixer, wooden spoon, flour, eggs, sugar, cocoa powder, spatula and other ingredients, I was now ready to make my first chocolate cake from scratch. I mean, what girl doesn't like chocolate. Following a recipe, I measured, sifted, stirred, mixed and made sure to use every drop of the egg by wiping the inside of the shell with my finger. Once all the layers were baked, frosted and put together, it was time to present my surprise masterpiece. Random toothpicks held the sliding layers from avalanching off the plate. With butterflies in my stomach, I was anxious and excited when I walked outside and presented my first baked creation. Mom was proud of me and it was a tremendous success!

One hot summer day, Aunt Cookie and Uncle Rick arrived with our cousins to spend the weekend at our lake house. Lake Zoar, a reservoir on the Housatonic River, was created by the Stevenson Dam.

Aunt Cookie would have preferred that the girls didn't go swimming because once their thick black hair got wet it was all that much harder for her to comb out. But we had a dock, a lake, and well, we were kids who wanted to play and swim. So we did! And at the end of the day, we shared our twin beds for the sleep over.

Soon after their visit, I spent a week at their home in Queens, New York and saw the sights; the Twin Towers, Statue of Liberty and the Empire State Building. Aunt Cookie introduced me to fried liver and onions. You can imagine my first reaction. Ugh! But as I grew, I grew accustomed to food challenges. I learned to like the liver and tolerated the onions, maybe because Dad wasn't forcing me to eat them.

One day when my sister and I were swimming in the lake, she panicked. Her eyes grew wide with fear as she stretched her neck high to keep her head above water. She had exhausted herself doing the doggie paddle. I swam towards her intent on doing something but had no clue what that would be. By the time I reached C.J. her fear had kicked into high gear. She grasped and climbed up onto me as she kicked, screamed and pushed me down into the water.

I learned that the thought of being rescued doesn't always relax a person. Rather it seems to make them stop holding their breath and panic all the more to be saved.

Mom recalled that she and Dad walked the edge of the lake shouting, "Don't fight it, don't fight it, go with the current towards the shore!"

> ...the thought of being rescued
> doesn't always relax a person.

Once the retainer wall had been poured to support the dock, family and friends were invited for a summer picnic. The kids challenged, dared, rushed and chased each other on the new wall. The object of the game; don't fall into the lake, but C.J. fell and landed on the rocks. She wasn't hurt bad but she got scraped and banged up. Our parents accused me of pushing her off the wall on purpose. C.J. defended my innocence, but they wouldn't listen to reason. Instead I was admonished before an audience of bathing suits, T-shirts and shorts then sent to my room for the rest of the day. C.J. acquired cuts and bruises and I received scars of confusion.

I wasn't sure what was happening. I was beginning to feel blah, uneasy, uncertain, disquieted, constrained. Big sister, babysitting, yelling, anger, chaos and Sandy had been dead three years. Combined with a home life that lacked edification, a mother who was on the fence and a Dad who was unapproachable, I stopped taking violin lessons by the time I finished fifth grade.

Was it the awkward age of ten? How could I know what it was supposed to be like? I only had one run at it.

Maybe kids will be kids. Maybe it was me. Maybe nothing was wrong.

And life went on. The mini skirt with go-go boots showed off my pre-teen fashion. Grandpa made us wooden stilts. I played tag football down the road and rode my bike with a banana seat and high handlebars. Mom dressed and posed us kids under the Christmas tree as Mary and Joseph while our brother, 6-days old, played baby Jesus. I cried when Mike's blonde curls were lopped off at his first haircut. Friends were made, but not with the boy who put worms on my head or the girls that pelted rocks at me and my sister when we walked home from the bus stop. Mom took us to The Von Trapp Lodge in Stowe, Vermont where we met the real Maria. I spent a summer week at Camp Wightman Baptist Christian Camp making new friends, learned to swim and made a cross out of nails. Back home I skipped down the imaginary yellow brick road and sang, "We're off to see the Wizard, the wonderful Wizard of Oz." Pursed lips squeaked, "Oil." Every June Mom took us kids to the Newtown Ice Cream Shop to celebrate the last day of school.

FOURTEEN

Serenity Lane

1974 - 1976 (age eleven and twelve)
House #7 ~ Serenity Lane, Sandy Hook

Serenity is the quality or state of being serene; clearness and calmness; quietness; stillness; peace. A general peace and serenity newly succeeded a general trouble, by Sir W. Temple along with Calmness of mind; evenness of temper; undisturbed state; coolness; composure, by Locke[14]

What is a raised ranch? Our seventh home. Some call this style house a split level. Dad built this home to sell, but it didn't therefore that's why we moved in. I was 11 and about to enter seventh grade. The first day at our assigned bus stop, C.J. and I stood at the corner of Bradley and Serenity Lane. Kids started coming from all directions and gathered on the other side of the street. From across the intersection, they stared at us making it obvious  we were the foreigners to the neighborhood. Taking in our new territory, along with potential friends or foes, we stood alone together and stared back. Moments later, I recognized one of the girls walking to the bus stop.

"Dawn?"

"Tam, what are you doing here?"

"We just moved to the neighborhood."

Phew! Finally a friendly face.

Dawn and I had met two years back in fifth grade when our reading classes were merged and called clusters. It seemed I had made a new friend. Little did I know when I talked her ear off during our silent reading hour she didn't have the slightest interest in what I had said. To clinch this new friendship, I noticed the seam up the back of Dawn's purple stockings and commented how cool it was. However, Dawn wasn't thrilled about my astute observation which brought attention to the fact she had stitched up a run with thread and nothing about this was decorative or cool. Embarrassed that someone noticed what she tried to conceal, we didn't become fast friends. With a polite nod of her head she smiled *you can leave me alone now.* She had tolerated me as long as she could. Clueless on my part, I gave her my phone number, but did not hear from her.

> Embarrassed that someone noticed what she tried to conceal...

Now two years later, much to my youthful excitement and her graceful dismay, we became reacquainted at her bus stop. With a polite conversation we tried, again, to exchange phone numbers on scrap paper. Sheepish, she promised that this time she wouldn't wash my number with the laundry.

I stepped into the school bus with a lighter bounce to my step because maybe this time we'll live in one home long enough for me to make a real friend.

Dawn's reservation soon dissolved as she warmed up to me living a few doors down the street. Our friendship grew as we rode bikes, played Monopoly, bocce ball or gin rummy in their pop-up camper. We could waste a day with young girl dreams and conversations that would solve the worlds' problems.

Now part of Dawn's family routine, I attended youth group at their Evangelical church and participated in Vacation Bible School. Like any good friend with a goal, I helped her finish Saturday chores so we could play outside. The biggest chore to get out of the way was the never ending laundry for Dawn's large family. Six people meant twelve feet. Mounds of socks were everywhere. It was a known fact that washing machines ate socks so I had to ask what their secret was to keeping pairs matched. Dawn stated, "We use large safety pins." Like the stitched run in her stockings years earlier, I thought this was the coolest thing I'd ever heard. Apparently, I didn't get out much.

Linda, a new friend from down the road had an endearing giggle. Her steady and calm outlook on life made her reliable. She no doubt received these traits from her parents; a mother who had a generous heart and a father whose eyes twinkled and made me feel safe. Not only did her mom open her pantry to me and my sister at any time, she fed day-old bread from the Pepperidge Farm outlet to all the local animals: raccoons, deer, fox, and any other varmint that walked on four legs. Fortunate for us, we were fed Cheetos and cookies. Whenever I played at her house, I'd see their resident owl sitting high up in a tree. It was remarkable how on any given visit I spotted the owl on the same perch sitting stiff and still. Her family educated me that owls are nocturnal and decoys might appear sleeping during the day.

But then when a bunch of girls get together, well that's a whole other story. It was the big neighborhood sleep over at Cathy's house on the corner. Amid girlish giggle's we changed into our PJ's and couldn't help but observe who were tall, short, thin or fat. Who had hairy armpits and hairy legs, pimples, were well-endowed or flat as a board or who had straight or curly hair? The list went on and on. We secretly assessed each other while silently questioning our own womanhood. Passing the cobalt blue jar to whichever girl dared, we scooped out white cold cream with our fingers and applied Noxzema to our faces. This cold stinging face cream with a medicinal smell promised to make us beautiful.

Days after the sleepover my girlfriend Dawn and I were taking an early evening walk down our street when she reported that one of the girls from the sleepover couldn't stomach me and I'd never be invited again. I looked at her perplexed.

"Whaddya mean she can't stomach me? What's that mean? Is there something wrong with my stomach?"

Dawn tried several different ways to explain it to me in kindness. I could be a little dense at times so I looked to my wise friend to spell it out.

"She doesn't like you Tam."

"What does that have to do with my stomach?"

"Tam, it means you make her sick to her stomach."

"What I do to make her sick?"

Dawn tried not to laugh. "Yeeesssh, ya didn't do anything, it just means she can't stand ya."

"Oh. That doesn't even make sense to say I can't stomach you!"

"It's a figure of speech Tam."

It was getting dark by the end of our walk which landed us in the vicinity of the sleepover house.

"Dawn, we put pajamas on and passed Noxemia around. How does that make someone not stomach me?"

"Oh brother, I probably shouldn't of told ya."

I looked over at the brown house, directed my anger towards the roofline and shouted, "Fine who cares, I never wanna sleep over there again anyway. Good riddance."

Then we laughed and ran home.

Junior high was an awkward time of life filled with a heightened awareness of who I was becoming. A time when I existed but didn't want anyone to know, yet I wanted the world to know. A sense like no one ever noticed me yet thought everyone watched me. A time to prove I had something to say, yet all my outward bravado screamed insecurities on the inside. Junior high was a time of chances, choices, consequences, coming of age and spreading my wings with blundering uncertainty in preparation for whatever lay ahead.

And as if that wasn't enough, I hated my teeth, my hair, my clothes and my body. I'd cover my mouth to hide my smile because two teeth were like fangs. At birth I had red hair that turned blonde in elementary school until junior high kicked in. Then my hair turned oily, straight and another shade of red. My clothes felt frumpy like my body, fat and ugly.

My sister and I played Monopoly in the family room and drank pre-made chocolate milk from a gallon jug while we negotiated high real estate deals. When we were bored with that, we created an obstacle course in the front yard with trash cans in an effort to mimic the Olympics.

Mom dusted off a small square box with a portable turntable inside and introduced us to forty-five RPM records. Each treasure trove from her teens held a single song per side and was inserted in paper sleeves to protect the record. We set up our DJ station on the fireplace hearth and pretended to wear poodle skirts with bobby socks for the sock hop. She informed us that girls of her day wore their cardigan sweaters backwards so the buttons weren't revealed in front. While we danced to music from Mom's youth, we learned repetitive lyrics to songs such as; "Splish Splash," "Come on Let's Go," and one of my favorites, "You Talk Too Much."

Dad and mom could be found at the kitchen playing cards or cribbage. Dad's eye squinted from the smoke of his Lucky Strike that hung from the corner of his mouth while he studied his cards. His round black plastic ashtray filled with cigarettes butts while a glass of iced tea sat on a coaster. Other times he played solitaire from the couch and used the vinyl hassock for a table.

I was sent back to Camp Wightman for one summer week which also meant a week away from my household chore of taking the garbage out. I was thrilled until I was assigned my chore at camp. Guess what it was? You got it. I swore it was a conspiracy. However, I qualified to swim farther out to the bigger dock which granted me rights to canoe to the island.

One year the maternal side of our family; grandparents, aunts, uncles and cousins challenged each other to be creative and make homemade gifts for

Christmas. Grandpa spoiled us with much of his craftsmanship as he turned a piece of wood into a functioning object. Collectively there were mug trees, spoon racks, jewelry boxes, pillows, candles, porcelain doll lamps, doll door stops and so on. I was proud of what I made; a dried apple doll scene of a wrinkled old couple. When put to the test to be creative, we had an amazing presentation. What a memorable Christmas.

In the mix was a variety of store-bought gifts. A boy cousin gave me my first rock album, Toys In the Attic by Aerosmith, released in 1975. I knew nothing about this band but loved the album because it meant I was older and cool. It moved me up the ranks from my Winnie the Pooh, Donny Osmond, Partridge Family and the Beach Boys Endless Summer albums.

One night I was stirred from a sound sleep when I heard the electric garage door open. Startled, I strained to identify the muffled noises that entered our home until I realized it was a person. From the safety of my bed, I followed the pace of the stranger who traveled up the stairs from the garage. Anxious, I listened to the foreigner walk around our house before moving down the hallway. Each step was slow, deliberate, and measured until it paused outside my bedroom door. My heart stopped until the feet passed by. Somewhat surreal, my sleepy state of mind didn't like this new sensation.

The next morning, sitting at breakfast with my family, I looked around the kitchen table and studied their faces for any sign of something wrong. Nobody looked disturbed. No one talked about an intruder or mishap in the middle of the night. It was business as usual as Dad stirred sugar and milk into his hot Lipton tea. We kids always remained alert while he steeped his tea bag. He'd start to take his spoon out of the mug and we'd flinch. Then he'd stir his tea some more and we'd giggle. The hot teaspoon game was his warped term of endearment. Whoever didn't move their hand fast got tapped with the hot spoon. We laughed as we grumbled and swore he wasn't going to win the next time. However that morning I wasn't in the mood. I was unsettled. I wanted to ask if anyone had heard something strange the night before, but I wasn't sure how to ask. Uncertain of the safety zone, coupled with the all too familiar knot beginning to form in my gut, I kept my mouth shut because I sensed the enemy closing in to take siege of our family.

During the mid-1970s the construction industry changed. Banks put a moratorium on loans which left builders like my dad with multiple mortgages to juggle. When Dad built the home on Serenity Lane as a spec house, the intention was to sell it. The day we moved in, my parents thought they had a buyer but it turned out to be a false alarm. We moved in because we couldn't afford two mortgages. As the loans crashed and the building industry became unreliable for a steady income, my father's mood and health grew even more temperamental.

When Dad came home he dragged the weight of his troubles with him. One day after work his body language strongly suggested he was on a mission. For a man with a limp, he came up the stairs rather quick and without uttering one word, walked into the hallway, pulled the phone off the wall and smashed it against the floor. Then he stormed down the hall and burst into our bedroom where C.J. and I were folding our clothes. God only knows what possessed us to do this, but we had decided to organize the clothes in our dresser drawers. Boring!

Dad's abrupt rage put a halt to everything. Without explanation, our drawers were hurled one by one across the room. Folded clothes tossed in disarray. One of the drawers skimmed across my dresser like a wooden torpedo. Before crashing to the floor it demolished everything in its line of fire. Although it happened in lightning speed I watched the porcelain doll lamp, a gift from our homemade Christmas, skid in slow motion and hover on the edge before she nosedived off the dresser cliff. It hit the floor with great force, and smashed to pieces taking any remaining warm thoughts with it.

Once the drawers were tossed I was next. Dad grabbed my arm and hurled me over my twin bed. And yes the floor was hard. Although it happened in a matter of seconds I wondered if I folded my clothes wrong or looked at him wrong. I knew better than to back talk him so I stayed on my knees and leaned on my pink flowered comforter until he left the room. There was no conversation other than we were commanded to go to bed. We had no idea what he was mad at, again, but we gathered it might not be a good time to ask or question his authority. We didn't utter a syllable, that was, until he left the room.

Boy was I livid. I'd had enough of his anger. My body ached. My arm hurt. Desperate this time for evidence, my sister helped me search every part of my body for a cut, bruise, something. Result? Negative. Other than a microscopic scratch from his silver stretch watchband, not one mark.

I was hurt, frazzled and sore. This time I wanted proof so bad I could taste it, but without wounds to show for it, who'd believe me? Because I never received a mark I began to question if I was really being abused.

I had no other life or family to compare this to, but something deep inside said this cannot be normal. Does everyone live like this? Do all parents treat their twelve-year-old kids this way?

> ...but without wounds to show for it...I questioned my abuse...

Much seemed out of my control. Life at twelve was already fraught with the daily navigation of friends and acquaintances, boys and girls who awkwardly noticed each other, teachers I liked and didn't like, clothes, oily skin, hair whose texture and color started to change, teeth that grew crooked, armpits that started to smell, hairy legs and locker room showers. And let's not forget the menstruation cycle, or as I was taught to say, "My monthly friend is visiting me." Well some friend, not only did it come at the most inopportune times and when I was unprepared, it made me fat and break out! Oh, and sanitary napkins were still attached with a belt. It was a war zone out there.

The mounting tension at home didn't bode well with the unstoppable puberty of youth kicking into high gear. I was tired of being yelled at, made fun of, hit, shoved, thrown, and beaten by his hands or his belt. I was tired of being the oldest. And I was tired because I could never figure out what to do right. The rules began to change daily. If this was love, it confused me and I no longer wanted any part of it.

One day this twelve-year-old had had enough. I ran away to Dawn's who lived a few doors up the street. Her mother was patient as she listened to my woes, then in her loving parental voice explained, "Honey you just have to talk to your parents. Go back and tell them how you feel, sweetie," as she assured me they'd listen and understand.

Begrudgingly, I went back home. Maybe it was sound advice to her, but if I couldn't understand my home life, how could she?

"A hot-tempered man stirs up dissension, but a patient man calms a quarrel."[15]

We lived on Serenity Lane yet it didn't offer any.

Food should be nutritious and sustain you. Bring joy and flavors into your life and dazzle your palate. Many of our family meals were tense and flavorless growing up. Some found their way to our floor as Dad pounded his anger into the evening meal. Other times we were charged with, "Hurry up or you'll get more."

To this day, I don't know why the plate of chicken cacciatore catapulted from the kitchen table and flew through the air before it collided with the white walls. The plate dropped, then broke when it landed on the tile in the entryway of our raised ranch as red orange sauce dripped down the walls. Dad stormed off and again, we had to clean up his mess.

Another time, after finishing a dinner that stayed on the table, we began the usual clean up routine by clearing the table. Dad barked at me, "Get your bone out of the garbage."

He had to be kidding. We'd already scraped plates from five people's meals into the trash bin. Thinking he was joking I laughed and continued with our chores.

Again, "Get your bone out of the garbage now! And finish eating your food!"

Regardless of what I discerned earlier, at this moment his eyes held a dark cloud casting out any imagined light.

In error, I hesitated too long. Like a boa constrictor, Dad lunged and grabbed the back of my neck and dragged me across the thick pine stained table like a human shuffle board, until my head was over the garbage. He shouted, "Get your bone and finish eating it!"

Held by the vice-grip of his hand, I dug through the garbage scraps and settled for a pork chop bone with little evidence clinging to it. I guess I was the only one who left meat on their bone. Once released from his grip, my disheveled hair hanging in my face, I finished gnawing on a bone as my family looked on.

I hate raised ranches.

I hate chicken cacciatore.

I hate pork chops.

In a state of survival, I learned to be an obedient child and eat everything on my plate.

I had already been told I was fat and now he nick-named me the family garbage disposal.

The lunacy of these messages became a lens that I viewed myself through. Regardless of what the mirror reflected, the wound penetrated deeper than the vanity of my outside shell.

The lie formed and shaped my view.

The lie fed my wound.

And the lie fed off of my wound.

It would be years before I realized that what is fat ...

is the lie.

What is fat is the lie.

FIFTEEN

A Bowl of Cherries

1976 - 1977 (age twelve)
House #8 ~ Sandy Hook

The summer of 1976 we left Serenity Lane and moved into the Riverside lake community of Sandy Hook Village. Our tiny rental house was up on a hill nestled among tall fir trees which blocked out most of the sunshine. The front door opened into the main living quarters. Look left, living room. Gaze right, kitchen.

During my school years, our family moved several times back and forth between Newtown and Sandy Hook. Even though we changed zip codes and elementary schools, I always thought the towns were one and the same. After all, the middle school for Sandy Hook and Newtown is located on Queen Street in Newtown and the only high school, Newtown High, is in Sandy Hook. Go figure.

During one of our many moves, a peer informed me that when I lived in Sandy Hook, I was on the wrong side of the tracks. To which I said, "I am?" Who knew there was another side of a track? In reverse, when people heard I lived in Newtown, they'd say, "Oooo you live in Fairfield County where all the rich people live." To which I'd say, "I do?" Our family's welfare poked holes in those silly theories because no matter which town we lived in, we went to the same schools, wore hand-me-down clothes, experienced food stamps and struggled to make ends meet.

Regardless of which county or borough or side of the tracks we lived, my concern was getting babysitting jobs and going to a friend's house to play. I never knew if my friends were rich or poor. My focus was to ride bikes, go duckpin bowling, roller skating at the Danbury rink, take walks, eat pizza and hang out with friends. As far as I was concerned, the town lines both blurred and connected us. Perhaps that was the innocence of innocence.

On the cusp of turning thirteen, I had a new image to grow into, my first pair of blue jeans. Denim represented freedom and promised to make me look cool, not dorky. After I wore holes out in my seat and knees I'd patch them stitch by stitch with different shades of blue calico fabric. I wasn't allowed to shave my hairy legs but I didn't care because I had my first pair of jeans.

My schoolmate Linda became fast friends with C.J.. To help celebrate my sister's birthday she brought a skateboard and slept over on our pull out couch. After a pre-teenager breakfast of Fruit Loops cereal, we attempted to skate but spent most of the day falling. Thank goodness our steep paved street was trimmed with guard rails which protected fruit loops like us from going over the edge. Our novice efforts earned us badges of skinned knees, elbows and bruised egos. However, my sister won the gold medal with her trip to the E.R. after she skinned her arm down to the bone.

Summer days waved goodbye as I was about to enter eighth grade. Somewhere along the way I became interested in drawing cartoons. I don't know if it was because of the Sunday comics or my Archie comic books, but I tried my hand at it and practiced on the variety of paper I retrieved from Dad's worksite. I created a portfolio made of construction paper to display my pencil drawings of Beetle Bailey and Archie characters along with a few Walt Disney animals. One day after school I was greeted by my maternal grandfather, Grandpa Gay, and Grammy Barbara who were visiting. I couldn't wait to show Grammy my art portfolio along with my prized possession, Beetle Bailey on canvas. Something stirred in me when I watched him emerge from a pencil sketch to green khaki paint. Grammy "Ooo'd" and "Ahhh'd" in her voice which was husky from years of smoking. "Oh darlin' these are wonderful, look how talented you are!" Her tone and the life in her eyes made me believe I was creative, special and loved.

One of the few times Dawn slept at my house, we drifted with the day as we walked and talked. Worn out from aimless chatter, we turned in for our non-sleep sleepover. Sharing my twin bed put us in such close quarters we were forced to talk some more until we remembered the bing cherries Mom had purchased earlier that day. We snuck down the little hall into the kitchen and helped ourselves to a sleepover snack of fresh red cherries still attached to their stems and poking in all directions from the bowl. As if we'd stumbled on a hidden treasure, we giggled our way through this delectable treat and plucked one cherry at a time. Our summer nightgowns covered our young budding frames. We stood in the tranquil night while the windows separated us from the dark mystery on the other side of the glass.

Suddenly our serene moment scattered when bright choppy lights broke through the windows like helicopter strobes searching for someone in the dark. They bounced up and down shattering the peace of our late night snack.

Startled, we hovered until we decided it must be a neighbor's car going home up the hill.

Instead however, in one fell swoop, the car pulled into our driveway inches from the house and parked. We stared like frozen ice sculptures on a dark summer night and watched as the headlights went black.

Panic set in however, and our hearts pumped fear as we ran back to the bedroom. With the gracelessness of bungling acrobats, we dove into my twin bed and whacked our bodies against the wall. Nervous laughter trembled as we pulled the covers up and over our faces. We knew not to speak as we heard my Dad enter the house. We held our breath and made every effort not to move or twitch. The silence was deafening. We could hear ourselves trying not to breathe. Our hearts pounded so hard Dawn and I whispered, "Can you hear my heart?" "Can you hear mine?" The tiny house felt smaller than ever, as if it was closing in on us like some Twilight Zone episode. As if the walls could hear us trying not to breathe while they closed in on us with each pounding beat of our hearts. We laid frozen in the moment so sure he'd hear.

SIXTEEN

Confusion is the Enemy

Why is it once babies are born, many parents have an innate sense that they need to instill something good into their children? Some know with clarity why they feel that way, while others aren't sure but they sense in their heart of hearts that they need to foster something good for the sake of their child. Or maybe it's just tradition and they don't know why they do it, but either way it may look something like a baby dedication, baptism or catechism classes. Whatever form it takes it seems people try to do something because they feel a need to protect or save their little one from something bigger than them.

In our case, when us kids came along, the Sunday church routine began. As early as three years old, my mother started bringing C.J. and me to church which introduced us to nursery school. We'd never been separated before, but the Methodist church wouldn't cater to mother's request to keep the two of us together so my two-year old sister cried. Mom, a young mother feeling the pang of being stretched, wasn't thrilled with their methods, but tried to make it work. Willing, she became involved and taught Sunday school with flannel-graph figures on felt board. Deacons paid Mom a visit to our home and admonished her, "You can't teach Bible stories like that. You have to follow our curriculum about sharing," and further informed her if she continued to teach stories from the Bible outside of the curriculum, she risked losing her volunteer position. Mom protested the rigid church lacking joy and switched us a stone's throw across the green to the Baptist church. She begged the woman who welcomed her, "Please don't separate my little girls, this is a new experience." Warmly she replied, "I wouldn't dream of separating them." Mom recalled, "That's when I knew I found my church home."

Our church, which was built in 1848, had Baptist in its name yet I was told I was a Protestant. Across the street was a Methodist church, and scattered throughout surrounding towns were Saint this and Saint that. Whenever someone asked what denomination I was, I didn't know how to answer. My understanding of a denomination was whether or not I had enough Monopoly money to buy up Boardwalk, purchase a RR or get out of jail free. With no understanding of the man-made distinctions of church, their definitions, or labels put on church goers, my confused response would be, "I'm Baptist, or Protestant. No maybe both, I think. I'm not sure."

Our Reverend, a nice gentle man, was as ancient as the hills. When he retired the church hired a much younger pastor who seemed to bring something different to the church. Soon after his arrival, the church ladies buzzed around doing what church ladies do, fussing and fixing, preparing and clucking while the rumor mill rattled on with idle chatter about the many ladies of the church who liked him. Rumor suggested not only was he a good listener, but that he went above and beyond his pastoral boundaries to comfort a few ladies!

For seventeen years Mom made a career volunteering as a Sunday school teacher, superintendent, deaconess, church secretary, the pastoral committee, the women's circle and she held Bible studies in our home. I have no memory of the bible studies or being invited.

Mom reported that Dad would come to church to watch us kids on special occasions. Other than the 1978 church directory photo, I have no recollection of him being with us.

The word was he was in pain or working to make ends meet. However, as the years went on, his reason for delinquent attendance changed. Dad, the head of our household, insisted we go to church with Mom while he attended his church held in the back rooms of our small town's casual eating establishments. It was a private off the books service so he could see the queen and raise her with a king. When the chips were down, so was he. His holy communion of pretzels and shots of whiskey offered no relief. Should he partake too much of his communion, his raised spirits could wreak holy hell for anyone in his path later that day. The only time the smoke from his anger cleared was when he paused to light up another Lucky Strike. Instead of taking God up on His offer to leave burdens at the cross, Dad chose to play poker face while carrying the weight of his burden on his own shoulders. His absence from our family on Sundays to play five-card draw was the only view I knew him to have of God.

I was dedicated as an infant, attended Sunday school since age three and by twelve I had attended classes to confirm my choice to be saved from Hell. Mom's handwriting inside the cover of my first Bible[16] revealed her efforts to guide me into a better direction. She inscribed my name, our church and my Sunday school teacher along with proof of my deliverance date. The floor of the sanctuary, where the minister preached and the choir sang, hid the baptismal pool. After being dunked in the water, I changed from the wet clinging white robe to the red corduroy jumper that Mom had hand sewn. The box pattern of little white flowers marching across my body didn't slenderize my view. Insecure and hating how my body looked and confused about who I was, I felt fat as I posed for the group photo that captured my salvation.

> I felt fat as I posed for the group photo that captured my salvation.

SEVENTEEN

The Grip of Confusion

(age twelve to thirteen)
Riverside Road, Sandy Hook
1976 - 1977

I invited Dawn to my junior high youth group which was held at our Baptist church. After her parents dropped us off, we entered the annex and followed the chatter into the game room. The new young pastor welcomed us and seated us at a table with a board game waiting to be played. No sooner had we settled in, a hunt for candles pursued. Within minutes I sensed Dawn's discomfort. She claimed she felt sick to her stomach then rushed out of the room crying. I followed her into the hall.

"What's wrong?"

"I can't play that game, Tam."

"It did feel a little weird but it's just a board game, isn't it?"

"No, it's a foothold for evil."

Still crying she charged, "It's bad enough they're playing with a Ouija board, but a séance? That's why they're looking for candles. Don't ya know this goes against teachings in the Bible?"

Disturbed and still shaking Dawn proclaimed she wasn't going back into the game room. Instead, she called her dad from a wall phone and asked him to pick us up.

Dawn, who was also raised with some church influence, seemed to have a different experience from mine. Her dad went to church with his family and they prayed at their dinner table, letting their conversations from the Sunday service influence their Monday through Saturday.

The foundation of my Christian belief was fractured. My home life didn't coincide with Sunday messages. As a rule, we didn't talk about them or pray. My father's form of discipline and iron fist seemed contrary to verses in the bible which suggest that fathers don't embitter their children, or they will become discouraged.[17]

Despite my cracked foundation coupled with a pastor whose principles seemed ambiguous, I wasn't willing to test the twinge of discomfort that had stirred in my gut. There was no way I was going back into the game room without Dawn.

Whether or not one believes in the mystique of the Ouija board and séances, what stayed with me was a glimpse of what protection looked like. From lessons Dawn had learned at home, her first reaction was that she sensed danger. Her second reaction, without hesitation or doubt, was she knew who to call. The result was her daddy came and he rescued her.

Throughout eighth grade C.J. and I would sit at the kitchen table doing our homework until Dad walked through the door. When his drinking increased, his new routine brought him home past dinner time. He would stumble in and shout, "You girls get outta here and go to bed now." Upon reflection, Mom recently shared with me that she had to write numerous notes to our teachers to explain why our homework was often incomplete. His drinking challenged her to come up with new excuses because there were only so many crises a family could have.

Because of my dad's heritage, I was proud to say I was part Italian until I learned stunod or stunat meant stupid and, depending on the dialect, stonato or stunatu meant out of tune. When I asked what a word meant, his retort would be, "Don't be a stunod and look it up in the dictionary." Well, if I was ever allowed to finish my homework, maybe I would have known how to use a dictionary.

And at the end of all of this, during a moment of supposed levity, my family, including me, would laugh at Dad's joke when he'd ask, "What's stunod spelled backwards?" After my sister and I tried to decipher the code, we were stumped so Dad and Mom laughed, "Donuts! Stunod spells donuts!"

During the summer after eighth-grade graduation a miracle happened. A cute boy appeared outside my bedroom window unannounced. Startled by the knock, but intrigued, I opened it. After all I had a crush on him. Eager to be liked, I listened and hung onto his every word as he went on and on about an up and coming entertainer who rocked his world. I could care less about the music, but it sure was nice to be noticed, so naturally I purchased the album in hopes he'd be impressed.

Summertime meant going to the local town pool, a public cement swimming hole painted blue, which held the residential snapping turtle people insisted they'd seen. No matter who you spoke with, the legend was, "Watch out for this huge old creature who's 100 years old or he'll bite you."

One day the same boy who had appeared at my window called and asked me to meet him at the pool. He said, "I have something very important to tell you." Plans were already in motion to go to the town pool with girlfriends so I figured there wouldn't be any harm in meeting him there, also.

We girls marked our spot on the lawn with our beach towels and lathered up with baby oil, the perfect formula for sunburn. But the warmth felt good. I hadn't told them that I was meeting a boy. I didn't think it was necessary. It was a crush, nothing serious. Besides it was going to be a quick hello to listen to his question. So when it felt right, I made my excuses to the girls, "I'll be right back."

"Don't be long Tam our ride will be here soon."

"Don't worry, I won't be. This'll be quick."

One of the girls had a built in swimming pool at her home where we planned to continue the pool party later. I sure wasn't going to miss that.

Following this boy's weird request and directions of where to meet him, I left the boundaries of the public pool and found my way into the outskirts of the woods, which surrounded the park. I walked further into the woods and wondered if I'd made a mistake. Concerned, I grew anxious and thought about turning around, but then he appeared out of nowhere, beckoning me towards him. Forgetting my hesitation, I lit up like a Christmas tree when I saw the boy who smiled back at me.

"What's up?" I'd asked, "What was the important thing ya wanted to talk about?"

He replied, "I want to show you something"

Okay, "What?"

Forgetting my hesitation...

He proceeded to unzip his pants and pull out his private parts.

My youthful glee turned to fear.

He told me what he wanted me to do for him while his voice remained calm and gentle.

My whole body started shaking and trembling, as I said, "No."

He told me this is what people do for each other, who love each other. He assured me it was okay to do this. I didn't feel okay, I froze. I was embarrassed being in his presence. I was confused and desperate to be loved, but deep down I knew what he suggested was wrong, but I liked this boy because I thought he liked me. I'd never seen boys' privates before and I knew I didn't want to do what he asked, but he kept saying if you want me to love you, if you love me.

The enemy not only lurks around in hidden dark crevices but on a bright sunny day at a town pool. He lurks, looking for someone who is lost and vulnerable. The enemy's goal is to devour anything in its path like a bulldozer in a construction zone. The enemy is not there to rebuild. Rather, to tear down and leave a person ruined.

> The enemy is not there to rebuild.

I became paralyzed. I thought this boy was cute. I thought he thought I was cute and that he wanted to talk. I had thought this would be fun. Now fear was mixed with the wrong impression of what love does for another person. I found myself in a situation which terrified me and immobilized me, making me question what love is supposed to look like. Tears streamed down my face. Numbness entered my heart. I detached from my body, from the scene. I felt confused, ill, dirty and ugly and somehow this was my fault. I must have brought this on myself. I wanted to run but I couldn't move. I cried in bewilderment at this disgusting act he forced on me as he kept saying it was going to be okay. I didn't feel okay or loved, rather violated. After he continued to satisfy himself at my expense, he wanted to go even further. Already defiled and in a state of shock I cried, "No more," collected myself, and briskly walked away.

Dazed and confused I walked out of the woods with a fake smile as if nothing happened. Looking for my beach towel and friends, I found one girl who had stayed behind waiting and wondering where on earth I'd been. I couldn't tell her because I wondered the same thing. Her older sister, who had waited with the car, drove us to our friend's house so we could continue our pool party.

When we arrived they were already sitting around the pool sipping lemonade. I walked across the patio towards them, but I felt separated by a hundred miles of a gross secret I refused to share. I mean, what could I say? Things like this weren't supposed to happen. Looking in their eyes was difficult as this new lie began to enslave me. I stood inches from the girls, but the invisible glass wall that stood between us made them unapproachable and me unreachable. I had nowhere to hide, nowhere to run and nowhere to cry.

I pasted a big superficial smile on my face and answered the barrage of questions; hello, I'm fine, summer's good, sorry I'm late, ran into somebody, can't wait to start freshman year. I felt like I'd been ostracized, but it wasn't them, it was me.

> ...the new lie that began to enslave me.

I had no hopes of being rescued so who could I tell that would understand? Unlike my girlfriend, Dawn, who knew she could call her daddy to save her, I knew I could not find protection or comfort at home. Experience had taught me, if I knew what was good for me, don't call. So I didn't.

Two hours earlier I was lighthearted and excited that a boy had a crush on me and wanted to talk. The day at the pool took me to a new depth of inner self-destruction. Another piece of me died that day. Already low from a broken home brewing with tension, anger and fear I questioned my value and self-worth whose fragility was now shattered into still smaller shards of loss. If I had any hope left for what it would be like to be loved or to be someone's little princess, I no longer felt its glow.

> My fragility was now shattered into still smaller shards of loss.

With the town park incident secured and stuffed in the deepest recesses of my wound, I would enter freshman year in a few weeks.

EIGHTEEN

Will the Reign Ever End?

1977 - 1981
House #Nine ~ Newtown

*C*obbler's kids never had shoes so why should a builders family settle in one home. Soon to be a freshman, we moved to Kay Lane during the summer of 1977 when the Eagles big hit "New Kid in Town," had climbed the billboards to number one.

By default, I couldn't help but wrestle daily with braces, boys, pimples and hormones, coupled with low self-esteem, home life, and the inner conflict that raged from the summer's unexpected occurrence.

None of the homes we lived in offered a solution to our problem. By the time we settled into our ninth home in thirteen years, my family was frayed and unraveling slow with each thread of sadness. Gone were the optimistic days of thinking this time we'll settle as a family and our life will get better. Instead, what settled in our home was the chain reaction of unspoken pain and grief of everyone's inability to mend, share, love, grieve, express, cry, apologize, comfort, care and speak of all that was broken in our family. Hope was always there, but now it was tarnished.

> We became
> aberrations of ourselves...

Our personal wounds distorted our sense of unity. We became aberrations of ourselves departing from within and away from each other. As we moved into what would be our last home as a family, what settled was indifference.

In the midst of our family storms, I was granted permission to get my first pet, a dog. What fifteen-year-old doesn't want a puppy? I'd have someone to take care of, and love, and someone happy to see me. One of my parent's drove me to an old home on Churchill Road near the Sandy Hook Center. After being introduced to the litter of puppies I picked the cutest one and held her on my lap for the ride home. I wasn't sure what to name her but I knew I wanted something unusual. Maybe it was because Dawn's dog was named Andre. I don't know, but I knew I wanted something unique so I asked Dawn's older brother for suggestions. He threw out Francesca which is Italian for a female. It resonated with me, but for some reason I was determined to spell it my way, Francheska. Don't ask me why! But it didn't change the fact that I was crazy in love with my dog so I created a birth certificate adorned with blue ribbons and named her Francheska Dawn. It was how my adolescent heart could honor my best friend and her family for welcoming me into their lives.

Doing what every teenager of the day did, I worked to save money for a car. Work for me was babysitting. Many neighbors counted on my services because I was reliable and available. Whether it was daytime or nighttime, a funny pattern took place with every kid I watched. Any child who had to take a nap was poked, prodded or stared at while they slept. If I didn't see their body move, their little nose twitch, eyes dreaming, or hands, toes and feet wiggle I'd brush their cheek, belly or back and touch their hair until they yawned, stretched, or turned over in their crib until I was satisfied that they were breathing.

I loved each child I watched as I made their lunches, held them, rocked and played with them. Others received the M & M reward for potty training. Some would color pictures for me and parents would give me a school photo to tuck in my wallet for a keepsake.

Among the many jobs I landed, one was a long-term babysitting account mid-way down Kay Lane where the dirt road changed to Washbrook Road. I was back in the very house where I once lived and for a moment my pride swelled, *Dad built this home when I was eight,* but the swell quickly diminished as I recalled my father's hands tore apart much of what he built. And soon I realized I wasn't trying to reminisce but repress this illusion of my childhood.

It was hard to imagine what a happy marriage might look like with a family of my own, yet when I babysat all these kids I dreamed and pretended because it seemed possible. But back at home I'd be reminded why it probably wouldn't work. The fact that I carried my Dad's genetics didn't help the situation. Should I ever marry and become pregnant with a boy, I had a fifty-fifty chance of passing hemophilia onto my son. Because of my experience, all that meant to me was giving birth to an angry person. Should I give birth to a girl, she would have a fifty-fifty chance of receiving the gene and becoming a carrier which meant she'd be faced with the same decisions I had. Therefore, I declared to a high school friend that should I ever marry, I never wanted to have children.

By the time we had moved to Kay Lane, the medicine Dad needed for his hemophilia had become available to keep in our home versus running to the hospital every time he hemorrhaged. As a result the bottom shelf in our family fridge was designated to hold Dad's new staple: little glass vials of factor VIII and sterile water. Because hemorrhaging was internal bleeding, we could never foresee when Dad would be laid up a day or a week with joint pain which could be debilitating for him.

His disorder had no regard for our family's daily needs or circumstances, although his anger probably didn't help either. I mean coming home drunk and passing out in the driveway wasn't the hemophilia's fault. Nor the time he crashed the pickup truck. One might argue that the pain meds didn't help him think clearly. Either way he soothed his physical pain with Darvon[18] and his emotional pain with booze. Combined with the crash of the building industry, we lived day-to-day, unsure what time our father would come home or if he'd be in a good mood. The one certainty was the daily strain of uncertainty.

Mom was getting on my nerves. I'm sure I was getting on hers too because our life was a mess. But it seemed every time I needed her and tried to get her attention she'd say, something like, "Not now, I'm watching M*A*S*H." Abused or not, kids are still kids and can be a pain in the butt, selfish, and act like the world revolves around them. I imagine at times it was hard for Mom to sift through the differences of normal and out of control. But for me, I was at my wits end. It seemed the television was more important. Conversations weren't deep. It seemed rather than listening to my concerns, she avoided the home front situation.

Many unforeseen battles in our home forced me to adapt new daily work-a-rounds adjusted for Dad's mood, tension, and the time he came home. These survival tactics revolved around him and became my new culture. Guarded. Thinking. Decisiveness. Movement. Noise. Quiet. There was no specific method or manual. I just lived each day in hopes I'd get it right that day. Was the T.V. too loud? Was it because I watched T.V. or because I watched it in their room while I folded laundry? Was I on the phone? Did he get a busy signal when he tried to call home? Did I look at him the wrong way? Did I look at him at all?

The parental responsibility of watching Michael and C.J. fell on me after school along with many traditional chores. Having responsibilities wasn't the issue. It was how they encroached with unspoken expectations. Their instruction was born out of growing pressure sprinkled with fear of the unknown. Did I do it right? Did I do it wrong?

The onus of my role fueled my own tension as I fought the demons fighting me. Acting the parent role I'd been shown, I ordered my siblings around, especially my brother. Whatever the directive of the day was, he became defiant, or so it seemed. Frustrated, I'd yell and scream, "Take your damn clothes to your room, why aren't you listening, just do what I say."

During this time of strife in our family, much was a blur. My focus was on my own survival, coupled with being a teenager, while our family was winging it. When I reflect

117

on those days, one of my regrets was not realizing my brother was only a little boy who was exposed to the same tension that my sister and I were. I wish I knew then how to sift through the normal pesky brother stuff while loving and hugging him through the family chaos. And I wish I knew then how to be a better bigger sister to my shadow. The weight the responsibility put on me left me cheated of days that should have been filled with exploration and creativity. Of days that should have felt safe no matter how rich or poor we were.

At some point, the thing we are fighting can become the only thing we understand. We can imagine something is not right, yet we don't know what can be different. In the moment of the very fight we are fighting, the fight becomes all we know.

> ...the thing we are fighting can become the only thing we understand.

I wish I had known how to find the field of promised peace and rest that would protect my brother and sister. The same field where the wild flowers mattered and where the little sparrows and chickadees of the air would never fall. But I didn't know how to find those places.[19]

Journal entry: Sept 2, 1979 10:50 p.m. (age 15)

Lately I've had thoughts of running away. The reason why isn't exactly something you can exactly pinpoint. I don't know what struck me to want to. Just all of a sudden it hit me. I don't know I guess maybe it's been building up in me so long it just finally came out. I finally realized I couldn't put up with it anymore. I know I don't get brutally beat like some other people but I'm not them, I'm me....[20]

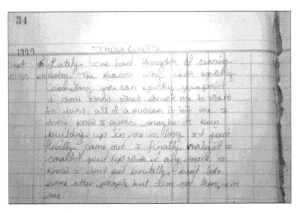

One evening I returned home after being out with a friend. When I entered the kitchen, the storm door closed behind me. With the weather still on my coat, I was sucked into the thick air which paralyzed me. My feet froze, stuck in the tension of fear. Life stopped as my heart quickened. I found myself facing the kitchen chair. Dad sat like an angry king with his arms resting on his throne of dark shellacked pine blocking the only other escape route out of the kitchen. I could have headed back outside, but I was too scared, and where would I go? It was dark. His throne, the all too familiar perch, is where he'd wait to pierce his prey with that icy cold stare when they walked through the kitchen door.

His eyes and tone suggested I'd done something wrong as he hollered, "Where the hell were you?"

"Out with a friend."

"What were you doing?"

"We were driving around."

"When I ask you a question you better tell me the truth, capiche? Where were you?"

"Just driving around with a friend."

"You fuckin nymphomaniac! Get the hell outta here and go to bed."

I was scared of his anger and confused about his accusation. I had no idea what he was mad at or what he'd just called me. When he was through with his tirade, he dismissed me like a jester who failed her king. Heading straight to bed, I hoped not to be beckoned back to his courtroom.

Dad's accusation left me unsettled making it hard to concentrate at school the next day. Like the encounter in the park a few summers back, a sense of shame and awkwardness washed over me. In high school you know you have to look cool and act like you know everything so I was embarrassed that I didn't know the meaning of Dad's accusation and I was afraid to ask. But at some point I mustered the courage and pulled my trusted friend Dawn aside. Huddled in the hallway as hundreds of high school students changed classes, I confided, "Man my dad was mad last night." Turning my head, I leaned in and whispered, "He called me an f'n nymphomaniac." Hopeful no classmate heard, I asked, "What is that?"

My jaw dropped when she told me. Although I'd grown accustomed to hearing the F-bomb at home, I was disturbed because both words together hurled a powerful hurtful punch at the value of who I thought I was. Mortified, I blushed, and then laughed. "Ha, I wasn't that, but I know girls who are," or so gossip implied. Man, what an idiot I was for not going straight to the dictionary. I could have spared myself the embarrassment, I'm such a stunod.

My own dad didn't know me, yet he believed the lie he made up about me. Okay, so it was another drunken stupor, but the growing list of messages I received about my image seemed void of any encouragement.

To alleviate the growing tension, I left the house a few times in the middle of the night. One of those times I walked to a girl friend's house. When I crawled in through her bedroom window her parents found out I was there and of course they weren't impressed. They allowed me to get sleep but wanted me gone first thing in the morning. I didn't blame them. After eight plus miles, I was midway down route 25, exhausted and limping when a car pulled up around 5:00 a.m. He offered to give me a ride which I declined but he insisted because he could see that my leg hurt. I accepted but remained guarded and held onto the door latch ready to jump out. I had him drop me off at the Botsford Drive-In so he wouldn't see where I lived. Another time, walking up Church Hill Road, I accepted a ride at night from a Corvette whose driver insisted I get out of the pouring rain. Today when I drive on Toddy Hill Road, a narrow winding street filled with blind spots, I wince and thank God no one hit me the times I walked that street in the pitch dark feeling lost and absent from my life.

Most days after school I hid in my room when Dad came home. But if he wanted something it didn't matter where I was. He announced his arrival by demanding, "You kids get down here at once!"

"Oh boy, what'd we do now?" All three of us ran to the kitchen and stood at attention.

"Do you see this?"

"What?"

"Look, open your damn eyes. Do you see now?"

"No, what?"

"The dent. The door is dented. Who put it there?"

All three of us chimed, "I don't know."

"I don't know? You don't know? What, does a ghost live here? Get the hell outta here." And we ran back to our rooms.

Because the proverbial "I don't know" ghost lived in our house along with three children and a drunken father, he was outraged. Forgetting the skills he learned from his trade of building houses, he tore the aluminum door from its hinges and carried it upstairs to my bedroom. I guess because I'm the oldest. From my bed, I ducked and blocked my face as he threw it directly at me then hurled my rocking chair. Both skimmed my red painted knick-knack shelf before hitting me.

I managed to come out somewhat unharmed, but not my knick-knacks. The animal collection of mommy and daddy dog families with their puppies, random woodland creatures, an elf, a bunny family, a penguin and unicorns were displaced. The St. Bernard who moments earlier had stood guard over the whole scene could no longer rescue anyone. Most of the animals were either shattered beyond repair or broken into chunks of pottery now in need of glue. Some puppies became orphaned. Woodland creatures were scattered and unicorns had lost their magic.

Once the whirlwind of my dad left my unfinished bedroom of two by fours still in need of sheetrock, I crumbled down onto my knees and wept. Discouraged, tears ran down my face at the mess in front of me. A cardboard shoebox would hold the broken body parts. One by one, I gathered my animals and held jagged pieces together to see who was repairable, who could live and who was beyond repair. Even the ones who might be glued would never be the same.

> Even the ones who might be glued would never be the same.

On my knees, legs sprawled out from under me like a fallen fawn, I continued reaching under my bed and in all directions for my scattered animals as I sobbed, "Life is tough out in the world so I guess some of you will have to go. Who cares anyway, you're only stupid little pieces of plaster."

I guess Dad was right after all. Throughout my childhood he had drilled into me, *Life is tough out there and my job is to toughen you up.*

After witnessing my silly cheap bric-a-brac dogs and their woodland friends shatter against the floor, more of me departed. Continuing to feed me was the insidious message of loss and unimportance. Why bother? Why care? Nothing has value so I must not be valuable. And I began to believe the lies.

Disheartened, my tears fell as I placed broken piece after broken piece inside the shoebox. The cardboard coffin became discolored and damp as my brokenness watered each shard, but no one came back to life. [21]

NINETEEN

The Twig Snapped

1979
House Nine ~ Kay Lane, Newtown

We lived during an era when it was safe enough to leave our homes and cars unlocked with a pocketbook or briefcase in plain view and windows rolled down. Car keys were left in ignitions, placed in the fold of the visor or under the floor mat. Our Connecticut cape was off the beaten path on a dirt road and yet it wasn't always safe to come home.

Another sunny day.

"Yay school is out!"

Then dread, "Oh, school is out."

The bus dropped C.J. and I off at the end of our dirt road. My stomach churned as I stepped onto the ground. We looked at each other, paused and then took a few steps toward home till we gained a clearer view of our driveway.

"Can you tell?"

"I'm not sure."

"Nope, don't see it."

Relieved that his car wasn't in the driveway we stopped holding our breath. Our shoulders slackened as the tension drained from our bodies. The lightness to our step returned as we ambled home talking about our school day.

We lived one day at a time as we breathed the afternoon bus stop routine. Get off. Pause. Look. Dread. Hold breath. Double look. Exhale.

Had his car been in the driveway, the uncertainty of his mood would have weighed us down and dictated the pace of our steps. And on those days the distance from our bus stop to our driveway was never long enough, yet it took forever as we walked the dusty corridor of broken eggshells.

Phase one, no car.

Phase two, the end of the day always came and he'd come home.

One typical day after school when dad wasn't home yet, we went about our business of homework, television, chores and dinner-prep.

> ...walked the dusty corridor of broken eggshells.

However, the afternoon game was afoot.

"What was that?"

"Did you hear it?"

"Did it sound like his car?"

"Can you see?"

"Quick, go look out the window."

"Is he home?"

"Yes!"

"Yikes!"

"Run!"

And run we did, up the stairs to our unfinished bedrooms, closed the door, and pretended to have been there all afternoon. We figured, regardless of his mood, we were out of his line of fire as long as we stayed quiet.

Leaning our ears against the door we stood still and listened....

It had been a beautiful sunny day in the New England woods. The birds singing were sheltered by the lush green leaves silhouetted by the bluebell sky. A gentle spring-fed stream flowed with crystal cool refreshment. The gentle summer breeze caressed the woods while whispering a perception of peace and shelter and safety. This private haven of life was secluded. The highway in the distance went unnoticed.

In the middle of the woods, a dense surreal quiet surrounded the fawns. Although they believed they were all alone, their instincts sensed life all around them in the primitive silence of nature which is loud.

After the fawns rested, they arose from their bedding to frolic in the woods. They heard leaves rustling. Their playfulness ceased. As if yoked, their heads turned toward the sound with hopeful assumption it was their mother. They continued to stare towards the disturbance with expectation. A doe will sometimes protect her fawns if the predator is small, but more often than not, the doe will stoically move on.[22] It becomes survival of the fittest.

The fawns continued staring into the void for their mother. She never came.

The disturbance of their refuge grew loud. Breathing quickened. They remained motionless.

Then there it was.

The twig snapped.

The woods fell quieter than the fawns. The breeze stopped its whispering, the birds their singing. Life became unnatural and still.

Muscles tensed in expectation. The fawns calculated their next move.

An explosion echoed in their heart throbbing ears, their refuge breeched. The hunter's shot rang out his command....

"Tammy Sue, get down here RIGHT NOW!"

Behind our sheltered door, my sister and I glanced at each other with silent words *what this time?*

Trembling, I opened the door and froze at the top of the stairs. I found myself staring down the barrel of his five-foot ten inch stature.

The angry hunter at the bottom continued to flush out his prey with verbal demands to come down stairs.

I did. One step.

Uncertain of my fate I stopped in my tracks. I wasn't exactly sure how close I wanted to get to the enemy at the bottom. Nervous, shaking and fearful of the glassy cold eyes that stared up at me, I held the banister for support. My legs became rubber. Nowhere to run and afraid of disobeying my father, I managed one or two more steps before the angry hunter lunged, grabbed my ankles and pulled me down the stairs to the landing. Then grasping his trophy by the hair he continued dragging me through the living room. Kicking and screaming, arms flailing, I freed myself from his grip. Words flew uncontrollably out of my mouth in defense of my attack as I shouted, "You fuckin' bastard!" Someone had to defend me, so I did.

Then the unthinkable happened. Still on the floor catching my breath, my mother, my witness, raised her arm to hit me for swearing at my father.

Any fumes of resiliency left in me or a willingness to make sense of this life evaporated and left the room. I'd become dispirited when she raised her arm. Our eyes locked. Everything in my head screamed; *this is how you protect me? This is when you find your backbone? You're kidding, right? You're really going to hit me right now?* No words were ever spoken but she must have seen the discouragement and hurt in my eyes. With perhaps a twinge of remorse, she lowered her arm, but she may as well have smacked me.

Mom's reaction blew my mind. Like, didn't she see what her husband just did? Was she really concerned at this moment with disrespect? If she even tried to wash my mouth with soap, I'd cram it somewhere. Wasn't I her daughter, too? Didn't I matter? Or was I just the milkman's daughter and the family punching bag? It hurt to be dragged down the stairs and dragged by my hair. What would it take for her to see there was a problem in her home? At that moment I lost all respect for her and any hope that she'd protect me.

I'd been minding my own business when I was attacked, but now I felt shame as I wondered what I'd done wrong. I no longer expected Mom to defend me or try to stop the madness.

Was my mother's action towards me in defense of her marriage vows, for better or for worse? Was I the worse? Was she going to hit me because I swore at her husband? Or was she about to hit me for having more courage to defend myself than she did? Perhaps her dream was not going how she imagined it should. Perhaps everything was wrong with her fairytale marriage and her Prince Charming. Maybe, she thought hitting me would strike order into her home that was falling apart.

To this day, I don't know what pissed off my old man.

TWENTY

Pasta, Squash, Beans & Strife

1979

Fifteen and angry for being dragged down the stairs, I called The Department of Children Youth and Family Services (DCYF). Perhaps a dangerous mission, but I didn't care what happened to me anymore. How could it get any worse? My parents were not thrilled I called the child abuse hotline, especially Mom. DCYF ordered our family to seek counseling. The tension of a state organization interfering and interjecting their view of acceptable family structure only caused her more grief. It overloaded her full plate and interrupted her efforts to keep peace in a home where there was none.

DCYF performed a couple of random home visits where they reported to find everything in order and our father in a good mood. Of course scheduling the pop-in appointments worked in Dad's favor.

While the DCYF ball was rolling, I wrote my mother a letter in which I stated, "My father comes home practically every night drunk, late or early, and causes problems," and "Maybe he does love me, but he has the damnedest ways of showing it. I'll keep in touch." I was so angry at my mother, hurt and confused at how she couldn't see what was happening. My scathing two-page letter remained folded in my wallet for years. I never did give it to her because in the middle of all that craziness, I still didn't want to hurt my mother. But I didn't want to be hurt anymore either so after I wrote it, I ran away and lived at Dawn's house.

Other than the couple of home visits by DCYF and a few family counseling sessions one of which Dad had attended, our case was closed because they found my claim of abuse unwarranted. However our parents agreed to let me continue to live at Dawn's for a while as kind of a cool off period.

Dawn's parents, now accustomed to me as a part-time fixture of their family, were willing to take me in and offer shelter from the storm. Three years had passed since my first S.O.S. No longer twelve, the family had come to understand my need for safety and respite.

Dawn's parents became Mom and Dad N. to me as I settled in with their family of six. Her Russian and Italian parents woke up my sense of taste as they introduced me to different foods; pierogis, blintzes, crepes, pasta, homemade pizza, for starters, and yuck, liver pate. And who knew pasta didn't start in a box? From scratch pasta was born along with Dad N's homemade mixture of Italian goodness which he put through a meat grinder and into sausage sleeves. The piece de resistance, was his homemade cannolis. Not much else to say. The word speaks for itself.

Whenever Mom N. asked if I'd tried a certain food, before thinking twice, I'd speak once and declare "No!" That was my way of stating, I hadn't tried it, thank you, but no thank you, not interested. I soon learned the word no should never be my first line of defense when it came to food because the word no was the only leverage Mom N. needed. If I had already tried a food I didn't like, she accepted that response. However claiming I didn't like the looks, smell, or color of something before I tried it didn't excuse me from her supper table. I soon discovered she had absolutely no sympathy for not trying new food.

"Have you ever had eggplant parmesan?"

"No."

I could tell immediately I gave the wrong answer because she was about to serve me a helping. Apparently I needed to explain more so I said, "I hate squash. It's soggy and I don't like the way it looks." Thoroughly satisfied that my explanation clarified this matter, I began to relax.

"Oh?" Mom N. declared, eyebrows cocked with her unwavering stare. Although her eyes twinkled, I was not convinced I had won.

I soon learned what everyone else knew; the house rules were being spelled out for me. Mom N's fixed smile made it clear, while sitting with her family of six as a guest in their home I was about to try eggplant parmesan. The table chatter ceased as everyone turned their attention towards my plate. "Oh boy, this is not fun," I muttered to myself.

Embarrassed, I shifted and re-positioned myself, utensil firmly in hand, I cut into my meal, blew on it, paused, smelled it, then put a forkful in my mouth while twelve eyes watched.

"Hmmm, not so bad." Between the spaghetti sauce, ricotta and mozzarella I couldn't even tell it was squash.

Relieved, everyone continued eating and the table chatter resumed. No one yelled at me, timed me, gave me another helping and no one threw the kitchen table upside down.

I think I was more excited to be Dawn's bunk-mate than she was to have me because my morning chatter started at the first sign of daylight. "How are ya? How'd ya sleep? What d'ya wanna do today?" She set a new policy in place and challenged me, "Tam, zip it, wake up and please be silent. I'm not a morning person." I'd wake up and tried real hard to say nothing but restless words got stuck in my throat so I stared at her until I could get her to crack. Exasperated, she barked, "Okaaaay, yeeeesshhh, go ahead, what?"

Living at Dawn's house didn't change the fact that teenage life continued. I attended her church and turned sweet sixteen under her family's roof. Regardless of my home life, I still had to go to school. Classmates didn't know I was living somewhere else but in my head I was sure everyone knew my secret, because I had one. Even my high school sweetheart, Don, didn't know. For a brief period, I tried to dodge him in the halls, but I knew I couldn't keep avoiding him. It would seem weird and unnatural. I mean, after all he was bound to call my home and ask if I wanted to take a walk or go to the movies at the town hall. I'd have to give him Dawn's number, but how do I explain why? Scenarios ran through my head such as;

"Hey, I'm living at our friend Dawn's house. Here's her number."

He might ask, "Why?"

"Oh because," I might say.

Yeah, like that would fly. He'd know I'd be lying. Kids are supposed to live with their own family. Ashamed, I wondered how to tell him I was dragged down the stairs. What if he looked at me like my dad did, like I'm the problem and deserved it? Or worse, what if he breaks up with me?

> ...but in my head I was
> sure everyone knew my secret,
> because I had one.

I laughed a lot so on the outside it appeared I had it together, but inside my adolescent world was falling apart. I milled around the school halls uncomfortable with the position I'd been put in but when I mustered the courage to tell him, he showed concern and loved me more.

Don was an outdoorsman who taught me about the different fir trees, spit-bugs and the various birds. His love of fishing was passed to him through the generations of his grandfather and dad. During an outing with his family it was my job to carry the bait. The only place I had to put the shiners was in my pockets. Dating this boy felt special, proper, honest and pure. Unlike my experience near the town pool, he never bullied or threatened. And he never forced himself on me. I had an innate sense which suggested this is what a gentleman is and this is how a girl should be treated.

His parents, who I called, Mr. & Mrs. G., embraced me as one of their own kids. My boyfriend's ethnicity was the same as my best friend Dawn, Italian and Russian. Bouncing back and forth between both places introduced me to a variety of home cooking that awakened my palate. The G's house had a similar food education program, in that if I'd never eaten something before, I had to try it once. Mrs. G's finger held more power than a magic wand. One look on her face while wagging that finger and I was sunk. Well, there was no getting around the fact that if I wanted to eat under her roof too, I had to try something new before saying, "No, I don't like the looks or smell of it."

What is it with the squash, here we go again! Baked acorn squash drizzled with maple syrup and spaghetti squash with butter, salt and pepper. My nose scrunched as my taste buds had a hard time envisioning squash as spaghetti, but much to my surprise it turned out I liked them both.

After school, I'd ride Don's's bus to his home. We'd cut a path through the trees that bordered his neighbor's property. Mrs. G. would greet us with homemade apple or peach pie, but the absolute to-die-for was her Father Sarducci Cheesecake.[23]

Every year Mr. G. planted a garden and without fail, if the deer didn't eat it first, I'd get to share in his bounty of tomatoes, beans, garlic, parsley, basil, Yukon gold potatoes, squash, and so on. He always called me his bean-buddy.[24]

For the two plus months I lived with Dawn's family, they'd thrown me a safety net filled with guidance and love in a home that offered me a reprieve from daily strife. But my escape was short lived. Dad wanted me home. Enough was enough and Dawn's parents weren't comfortable keeping me against my father's wishes so back home I went.

And life went on. Boyfriends, girlfriends, braces, junior prom, anti-senior-prom party, babysitting, bought a ten-speed bike and then the cars came. Because I'd been working the neighborhood babysitting, I had saved enough money to purchase my first car, a used gold Datsun. My choice to get a foreign car stemmed from hanging around Dawn because her dad, Mr. N. repaired radiators out of his garage. His knowledge of cars had his family driving Toyota's due to their longevity so he suggested a Datsun would serve me well. Using my hard earned money, I purchased and gassed up all my used cars which included a Duster, Tempest and the most expensive, the Pontiac Firebird. They ranged from two to eight hundred dollars. And as life continued, I snuck out of the house to play penny-ante poker. Loved taking pictures and making spaghetti sauce. Drew cartoons and sewed pillows. Friends played guitar. I listened to music by the Doors, Lynyrd Skynyard, Simon & Garfunkel, Jim Croce, Mamas & the Papas, CCR, The Grateful Dead, Carol King's Tapestry, and the Allman Brothers and so on. Mom took Michael to his Cub Scout father and son soap box derbies. C.J. hung out with her friends or mine. Dad introduced me to escargot and invited Dawn and me to a clambake. He challenged me to eat raw clams on the half shell and slurp them down with hot sauce. By god, I was going to like them, and did.

TWENTY-ONE

I Guess it's Not Abuse

1979 - 1983

In spite of the turmoil in our home, creativity managed to find its way out of me in desperate, timid spurts in order to prove I existed. Because many of my high school classmates played guitar, a new interest emerged, along with the hope that Dad would teach me how to play his acoustic and electric guitar. I assumed he would be pleased if I showed an interest in learning about something he enjoyed so I asked Mom if she would resurrect the old song sheets from his early jam sessions. I shared these with a girlfriend and asked if she would teach me how to read some of his favorite songs so I would be prepared. She taught me the basic chords that were on the sheets.

One day when it felt right, I approached Dad who

was sitting on the couch in the living room and asked if he would teach me. Without skipping a beat, he unapologetically said, "You never stuck with the violin, why should I teach you the guitar?" So he never did.

I felt deflated and embarrassed. I felt stupid for asking because I should have known better. And worst of all I believed he was right. So I never continued to pursue it.

It always seemed I was holding my breath for something good to happen but then the lack of oxygen would cut off the art of who I was trying to become, whatever that might look like. It suffocated everything in me that was waiting to grow and bloom naturally. Like a pest that irritated someone's neck on a hot and humid summer day, my spirit was squashed.

While the chasm grew wider at home, sharper edges of the eggshells dug deeper and deeper. I held my breath more and more until I withered from the confusing messages I received. Speak. Don't. Cry. Don't. Be. Don't. Messages, when translated, said *you can't do anything right and nothing you have to say is important, so why bother.*

So I said nothing. That is, nothing that was real. I was breathing, but inside I was dying.

Living with Dad was like playing Russian roulette. I never knew what would make him pull the trigger or when his bullet would strike. Was he content? In a good mood? Or at least was he in a non-confrontational mood?

Did I fold the laundry wrong? Did I let the door slam? Did I question the food on my plate? Maybe I didn't eat it fast enough. Did I put the butter away? Did I? Did I? Did I? Tip toeing around these mind games exhausted me. I wanted to be under his radar but I felt like a moving target.

Fear gripped me in new ways leaving me vulnerable. The fear of being grabbed or dragged hid on the stairs or lurked in the dark corners of basements or anywhere dark. Fear hid in the woods. The fear of being hit was everywhere. It was behind me if I didn't have a wall to protect my back. It hid under my bed because I didn't know what was there. Going to bed became a chore because I feared the edge. I paused, lunged, jumped, and rolled into bed. Fingers and toes tingled for fear of being grabbed by the darkness underneath. Once in bed, no extremities were allowed to hang over the edge of the black hole. They recoiled to the safety zone of the mattress before they could be grabbed by the unknown. As if putting invisible armor on before falling asleep,[25] I turned my back against the unfinished two by four bedroom wall so I could face the entrance to my room at the top of the stairs. I tried to fall asleep and shut down the fear of his unexpected wrath.

On the other hand my sister wondered what was wrong with her because she didn't receive the glowing attention I did. She'll laugh, "The only attention I got from Dad was when the T.V. flew over my head. Good thing I ducked!" She forgets to mention the time she fell on the ice, broke her leg, and had to wait for Dad to come home and eat supper before someone took her to the hospital. Not to mention the time he was mad and chased her through the house where she ran, slammed the door and cowered behind the toilet.

My conversations with my mom became brusque. I could not understand why she stayed married to this man. After I was made to come back home at 16, I didn't feel like I belonged to this family nor did I feel wanted. I didn't know why they made me return. I threatened Mom that if she didn't divorce him by the time I was 18, and of legal age, I'd leave. But guilt would accompany me over this because divorce was not the preferred method and he was her husband after all. It's just that he wasn't mine. He was supposed to be my dad and I didn't understand any of this.

I refused to wish them a happy anniversary. It was all bullshit to me. I felt bad for my mom, but I couldn't support her any longer. The tension grew between us as I insisted she choose between him or us.

Journal entry: August 30, 1980 12:10 a.m. (age 16)
Mom's decided that 9:00 a.m. Wednesday morning Dad should get served. Tonite I went to the Barn with the youth group. It was fun. Afterwards we went to "John's" for pizza. I tell ya – I hate life a lot. Things just don't seem rite no matter what....[26]

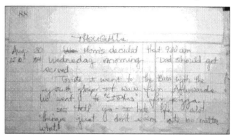

Journal entry: August/September 1980 (age 16)

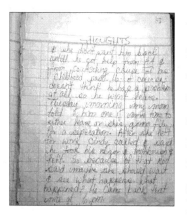

...& she didn't want him back until he got help for AA & from counseling cause of his childhood past. He – of course – doesn't think he has a problem at all so he won't leave. Tuesday morning my mom told him one more time to either leave or she's gonna file for a separation. After he left for work, Cindy called & said he took his razor & toothbrush & left. So because of that her attorney said maybe she should wait & see what happens. What happened? He came back that nite at 6p.m.[27]

Our messy home life turned everything upside down. Everything that was wrong became standard. It was hectic and tense. I was tired, lost and had headaches. The turmoil of our new normal left us all with different recounts of Dad's rage. Like how many times he threw us out of the house. Mom said once. I insisted at least twice. C.J. doesn't know. My brother was too young to remember.

> Everything that was wrong became standard.

After dropping us girls off at choir rehearsal Mom went home, walked in, and was thrown back out. She had looked at Dad the wrong way. She then drove back to church and arranged for my sister and me to spend the night with parishioners. Unsure what to do with Michael who was still in the house, she parked down the road from our house out of sight. She was unable to sleep as she tossed and turned in the car from the cold October air. After a few hours, she gathered the courage to go back inside the house. The antagonistic kitchen greeter barked, "Who told you, you could come home?" "I did," and she went to bed.

On another occasion, the head of our household was in a foul mood which forced another impromptu sleepover in the middle of the night. Mom began to load us kids up in the car to take us somewhere but I refused to go because now I was angry. I shouted, "I don't care where you go, I'll find my own place to sleep." She drove off while I walked down the dirt road to a schoolmate's home and knocked on

Nancy's door. I revealed that our family had been thrown out of the house so I asked if I could I spend the night. She asked me to wait in the kitchen but I could overhear her plead my case to her parents in the other room as she tried to convince her father I wasn't some loser classmate showing up drunk or trying to sell drugs in the middle of the night. Reluctant, he let me stay.

"You drive the women of my people from their pleasant homes. You take away my blessing from their children forever."[29]

The message I received throughout my youth was that my life wasn't so bad and it could have been worse. Well this is true, something can always be worse, but does that make it okay and if this wasn't abuse, what was it?

Maybe it was just another bad day and this is how families are. My parents made it clear they provided a roof over my head and put food on the table. That is, when it wasn't being turned upside down.

I mean, to put it in perspective, anger, yelling and tension aren't physical. Name calling, verbal attacks, constant devaluing, well those weren't physical either, so suck it up cupcake. How was that abuse? Sure, I was pushed, shoved, hit, dragged and thrown, but nothing broke, on me that is.

The time me and my sister crouched in the bathroom with Mom, while Dad smashed glass on the other side of the door, was really just a drill for finding shelter in the event a real hurricane tore through the house.

So what if Mom didn't protect me. She worked and hand sewed my clothes.

So what if my father didn't hug me like his princess. He worked when he wasn't laid-up from his disability.

The beating on my bare bottom with Dad's hard calloused hand, belt or buckle was to ensure I didn't wet my underwear. There was nothing humiliating about being bent over his lap, my privates exposed, numb and red as I cried. That was his parental guidance.

I mean, had I ducked quicker, the flying door and rocking chair wouldn't have hit me. That was my problem. And if I came down the stairs faster, he wouldn't have had to grab my ankles. It was my fault for being slow.

Nobody told me I couldn't have friends over, but because my day to day seemed unpredictable, it was rare when I did.

Because Dad drank and gambled in the back room of his Sunday club while Mom taught Sunday school was no reason for me to be confused.

And the bone in the garbage? We were poor. I was wasteful.

The suppers took more abuse than I did.

The cold penetrating icy stares were his bad day.

The physical and verbal attacks were his parental wisdom.

When he threw his family out of the house, I guess he needed space. After all, he was the head of the household, his prerogative. What abuse?

This unforeseeable life strained my two-year relationship with my high school sweetheart. We never fought, we just talked marriage. However, by 17 the constant craziness of my home life gave me pause as my parent's marriage disintegrated. Of course I wanted to be

143

loved but I couldn't imagine being a good wife or a good mother. I knew I didn't want chaos nor was I intent on looking for it. I didn't want to be hit, only loved. Although I had no desire for strife, it seemed, I couldn't understand what to do without it. I'd grown accustomed to my family culture which seeped into my blood stream. It would take much more than being out of the strife to begin repairing my damaged soul which was a mess. I couldn't imagine what a happy married life should look like.

Journal entry: April 12, 1981 10:36 p.m. (age 17) Breakup with high school sweetheart) Tomorrow will be our first day of not going out. Yes, we're breaking up. This so called perfect couple (of course we didn't literally mean perfect – there's no such thing) are going on a temporary break up that could lead to permanent....[28]

My boyfriend and his parents did nothing wrong and I am forever grateful for the love and peace they showed. The climax of my family turmoil deteriorated the peak of our courtship until it became a casualty of our family's war.

If I lived in a mansion, there would have been nowhere to
run
His silent wrath suffocated the air in any room we shared
My heart palpitated echoes in my ears, reminding me I
must be alive
Yet no voice in the echo protected me or told me to run and
hide
I'm frozen in my body which feels detached from who I am
I'm frozen under the guidance of the overseers of my
childhood
Frozen with confused fear at my parents' unwarranted
anger and absence
A piece of me begins to die and detach from the
disconnected family
I lose who I am before I even know me
In the chasm of my mind with nowhere to go
I'm trapped on the inside of me
While standing outside of me
While in search of me
I feel stuck
Disengaged
I do not sense I belong to me or belong to existence
An indescribable sense of separateness from my physical
body connected me to my incompleteness.[30]

*"Exploit or abuse your family, and end up with a
fistful of air; common sense tells you it's a stupid way to
live. A good life is a fruit-bearing tree; a violent life
destroys souls."[31]*

TWENTY-TWO

The Aftermath of Confusion

When I was six I had a remarkable flying experience. With my arms spread wide and my body horizontal and poised, I looked left and saw my house on Aunt Park Lane and then I looked right and saw the swamp where the turtles lived. I was at peace when I flew, not above the trees or rooftops, but midway like a hawk in the woods of Maine near Grand Lake Stream. I glided effortlessly in the gentle breeze, amid the tender trees, taking in all that surrounded my scope. Amazed. Vivid. Calm. Peace. Freedom. Hope.

In junior high I flew again, I thought. Maybe. Uncertain. Hazy. Doubt. Determined to recreate the first time, I walked up Serenity Lane until our house was out of sight. At the crest of the hill, I planted my seventh grade feet and stood still. With effort, I psyched myself into the old flying sensation. I lifted my arms from my side and with measured movements skipped down the middle of the road. I felt clumsy and awkward, but convinced that if I stayed in rhythm, I'd glide. It didn't work. I felt silly. Alone in embarrassment I blushed. I couldn't get back to where the turtles lived. I couldn't find Serenity.

At eighteen as a bride's maid of my first girlfriend to marry, I posed with the wedding party on the front stoop. We captured her delight on film as we fought the April wind blowing our Gunny Sack dresses. The photo proved I stood in their yard, yet I faded during the festivities. A strange sensation swallowed me into its warped bubble.

Separated from the party, I wondered if anyone else got hit with such waves of disconnection. I even asked, "Do you ever feel like you're here, but you're not?" Blank stares said it all so I tried again. "Like, I mean, have you ever felt vacant from your body, like you know you're physically here but you're outside of yourself?" Again, polite but perplexed faces indicated no one understood what on earth I meant. What an idiot! How stupid of me to ask! Was I going insane?

I felt Trapped
I couldn't reach the turtles
I couldn't reach serenity
I couldn't reach me
My wings were now clipped[32]

Journal entry: 1982 (age 18)

My parents finally divorced. My dad and I still never speaking.[33]

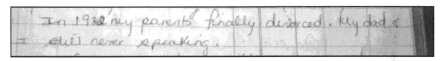

1983

The year of 1983, my family was shattered and scattered and finally divorced. Mom was preoccupied with her hurts as she prepared to move herself and our ten-year-old brother to California. She'd say my sister and I could have come with her but she wasn't really inviting us. Mom was distracted and unavailable for us girls. C.J.'s heart was broken when her fiancé left her after a three year engagement and my heart was grieving a friend who had just died in a car accident. What a mess. We were all a mess.

I was distraught when I attended my first friend-funeral that September. Minutes from home, Brett was about to get off his exit when the car he was driving hit road debris on the highway. He was in ICU for three days before he died. Part of my pain was I never had a chance to visit him in the hospital because I didn't know he was there. I learned about it after he died. Prior to the funeral I'd never met his parents. When introduced in the receiving line, they lit up, "So you're Tammy Sue? Our son always talked about you and your friendship with favor. We're so glad to finally meet you." We hugged.

Brett's grief-stricken parents invited me to live in their log cabin, perhaps to fill their void. Mr. & Mrs. P. was what I called them. Because my mother was preparing to move, I accepted their heartfelt offer to stay in my classmate's room, whose home I'd never been to. She brought me upstairs to help situate me in his bedroom and introduced me to their intimate world of loss.

Mrs. P. gave me her son's Boy Scout aluminum frame backpack along with his mess kit which had his initials B.P. engraved on the bottom. Maybe she thought I could use these because I'd recently returned from three-months of living off the land in the Ozark Mountains. I had stayed with my Sunday school teachers who had moved there to build their solar home. It was an exciting adventure where I milked cows, chopped wood and syphoned water into the house from the upper pond so we could bathe and do the dishes. In fact the last time I'd seen Brett was when I hiked with him and his best friend, Don, at Kent Falls before I left for my twenty-two hour bus trip to Compton, Arkansas.

After we went through the backpack, she picked up an envelope, "When going through my son's things, I found this letter he wrote to you but I guess he never had a chance to get it in the mail." We stood at the foot of his bed where she clutched the letter in her hand then held it to her chest. "I think it's only proper for you to have this. After all he wrote to you."

Stoic, she handed it to me as if it were a fragile baby bird's egg that had fallen out of its nest. We took turns holding it, then read it and surmised that this was the last letter he ever wrote. Knowing he was dead, it was surreal to look at his hand writing. After the Kent Falls hike with him and Don, I had left for Arkansas and they left for their big epic trip to California. The letter and the enclosed photo of them detailed the fun they'd had. It was weird. I tucked the letter into an old green ammunition box[34] where I kept my special memories.

Mrs. P. then looked over at a potted plant on a windowsill and explained how her son loved this spider plant. "I'd like to give it to you if you'd like to have it." She was a proud mom who was sad. I accepted without hesitation. The thought of having a piece of life from a dead friend offered a different kind of comfort.[35]

Mr. and Mrs. P's cabin offered rest and allowed me to keep my job at Andrea's Bakeshop, the local Italian bakery in the center of Newtown. How I loved working for those guys, Phil and Perry. Dirty baking sheets always in need of scrubbing. Counters to keep clean. Cake orders to take. Boxes to fold. Display cabinets to keep free of flies and windows and chrome to shine. Eventually I learned the regular customers and their cars as they pulled into the lot beginning at 6:00 a.m.. I loved the challenge of having their orders waiting for them on the counter as they walked through the door. Black with one sugar and a powdered donut. Cream no sugar and a cinnamon crawler. Light and sweet with a toasted poppy seed bagel and cream cheese.

Andrea's Bakery was hard and honest work laced with respect and old fashioned humor during a time when people could joke and everyone knew what everyone meant and no one was offended.

Once situated in the cabin I called Mom to check in.

"Hi Mom, how ya doing?"

"Hi Tam, I'm pretty much packed. Just a few more details to take care of before your brother and I head west."

"When do you think you're leaving?"

"In a couple weeks, around the first of October. How are your new arrangements going?"

"Great! I'm all moved in and I'm a lot closer to work."

"That's great. What about Francheska? Can she live there with you?"

"No, that's the only problem, they don't allow dogs so I don't know what I'm gonna do."

"Perhaps your father would be willing to help out and take Francheska. Why don't you call him?"

What an absurd statement. I couldn't believe what she suggested. Just because they were getting along better since they divorced didn't mean I wanted anything to do with him. But after I calmed down I realized I still desired to be loved and valued, so I took a risk and called Dad at his rental in Sandy Hook Center. Surprise of all surprises, he welcomed my call and said he'd be happy to care for Francheska until I found a place. I was shocked, yet relieved, that he offered. I mean, I never thought he would, but I learned miracles do happen. He invited me to his friend's house where he rented a room so we could talk about it. Although it was awkward, we sat at the dining room table and chatted. I felt like a stranger trying to get acquainted with the father she never knew, but I accepted the moment and settled into something out of the ordinary.

When Dad remarried, he moved to Stratford with his new wife and my dog. Random visits formed an unexpected father-daughter relationship. It wasn't flawless but it was unlike anything I experienced growing up. Perhaps it wasn't too late to begin healing the first 20 years. Perhaps it was strange that I'd be interested in repair when that mess and confusion were all I knew. But hope will have its way, if I let it, so I tried again.

> ...hope will have its way, if I let it,
> so I tried again.

1984

February of 1984 our family was divorced, separated four months and experiencing its new normal. I'd never been to California before so I took my vacation and visited my family. Mike's enthusiastic embrace about knocked me over when I walked into their new apartment. It was great to see my brother and awkward to see Mom. She was always happy to see me, however, our conversations now avoided the train wreck left behind so we maintained with surface talk. But it was a fine visit. I got to spend time with my grandparents and see the tourist sites of San Diego before going back home to my dead friend's room in the log cabin.

Journal entry: 1984 (age 20)

Now I have quickly summarized you on some things in the past 5 years. One thing important that I forgot to mention was, in 1984 my dad and I started talking because he took Francheska (my dog) to live with him. Since then, our relationship has <u>most</u> <u>miraculously</u> developed and we are close and even hug and kiss and say I love you. Anyone that knew me long ago knows that is a miracle....[36]

After I returned home from my vacation, Mom called one night to run something by me. "You and your father have been hitting it off lately, right?"

"Well, yeah. Why?"

"Would you say your dad's a changed man?"

"Changed? I guess he is because we're getting along okay. I mean, he seems different."

"What's his wife like?"

"She seems nice enough. I mean we can talk okay and she doesn't seem to put up with his crap."

"Does he still drink and does she?"

"Uh yeah ... I've noticed drinks around the place when I visit. Maybe that's why they get along."

"Do you think they have a drinking Problem?"

"I don't know Mom. What's it supposed to look like? What are you getting at? I mean, he remarried, so I guess he's lovable. He's watching my dog, so I guess he's different. He likes me now so I guess he doesn't drink like before. Sure Mom, I guess he's changed. Why are you asking me this stuff?"

"Because I've been thinking of sending Mike back to your father's for the summer. I can't be the male role model he needs. So whaddya think?"

"Well I mean I guess Dad's changed. I guess it's okay to send him back."

Even though Dad had been unavailable for much of Mike's earlier years, since the divorce, Mom began to realize that the absence of a father figure in her son's life had made a difference. She discovered that being a single parent while raising a son had its challenges. Mom recalled that after the divorce, she and Dad started getting along in a fresh way like old friends. With that in mind she thought Dad's new life and wife might offer a better balance for Mike than what she could have provided at that time. So she sent him east to live with Dad and his wife, the step-mother, for a test run during the summer of 1984.

Living with Mr. & Mrs. P. offered solace, as we both grieved the loss of their son. They for obvious reasons and me, because throughout our platonic friendship he had treated me like a lady. He must have learned that from his parents because they shared their son's good character and then some. However, shy a year of living with them at their tranquil cabin, their tender hearts still grieved the tragic loss of their only child so they moved out of state.

Fall 1984

As fate would have it, I'd been dating a young man who lived with his father. They had a pig, dog, chickens' and offered me and my dog lodging at their home. I moved into what resembled a father and son bachelor pad. Settled and employed at a lumber yard in Litchfield County I saw an end to an old life. Ready for a fresh start and excited to get my dog back, I called Dad about my new rental, "When is a good time to pick Francheska up?"

"There isn't one, you can't have her." Dad informed me that my dog would stay with him and his new wife. His statement was absolute. No question. No consideration. No option. No concern. No nothing. Just no.

Sure I may have been a little naïve, but Dad's response surprised me. He broke our agreement and basically kidnapped my dog. Unfolding in milliseconds like an old familiar screenplay, I was transported back to a digression of thoughts that questioned my confidence.

Did I imagine the plan?

We said temporary, didn't we?

The sickness of the old days built on power, control and bitterness seeped back in degrading the birth of our new father-daughter relationship. Another brick was placed in the wall I thought we were tearing down. In an effort to preserve what precious little we were building, I decided to swallow my voice again, with hopes this too shall pass. I acquiesced to the authoritative voice on the phone that said, "No." He kept my dog. I kept my dad. It was never mentioned again. The daily routine of work and responsibilities turned mundane shades of gray. Civil visits continued while my dad and his wife drove an unspoken wedge into an old wound.

In the meantime, my living arrangements changed from favorable to unacceptable. The novelty wore off as the empty cases of beer cans piled up in the garage like trophies in a competition between my boyfriend, his buddies and his dad. When my boyfriend preferred another woman, he broke up with me. His father viewed this as an opportunity to make unfatherly advances towards me, which I denied and firmly refused. I was no longer comfortable being there, but I had yet to find a new place to live. I felt trapped and desperate to be freed.

All that I knew had crumbled around me. My family was broken and separated by three thousand miles while my sister and I floundered. My friend was dead. The P's moved away. My rental accommodations fell apart. My relationship with Dad became strained and he kept my dog.

This wasn't the picture I had for my early twenty's. Engulfed in my grief, Dad's early life lessons came back to haunt and taunt me. Was he right that life is tough? Was I floundering because he didn't toughen me up enough, or was I sifting through the sins of my father's version of parental guidance?

1985

A pea soup fog settled over our family's divorce. It caused cloudy vision, and stunted clear thinking. Brokenhearted, I planned my second trip to California to begin damage control on my relationship with my mother. But in the meantime, my Litchfield life needed to be stored. Dawn held onto Brett's spider plant for me and my now ex-boyfriend's father offered his attic to keep my personal belongings. He said, "There's plenty of space for you to store your things, they won't be in the way. Take as much time as you need to get back on your feet." I felt he extended an olive branch due to his desperate but unsuccessful behavior towards me so I was thankful for the provision.

Once in California, Mom shared that she might send Mike back to Connecticut for a full school year because he returned unscathed from his 1984 summer-trial-run. She had prayed and sought counseling to help her discern what to do. The professional west coast advice concluded: send him to live with his dad. East he went while I continued to visit with Mom.

Still licking my wounds from the Litchfield breakup, I met who I thought was my dream come true. A dance at the Circle-D Bar and we were smitten. After a handful of dates, then a promise ring, he boarded his ship for Westpac, a six-month deployment in the Pacific where sailors cross the dateline. Still engulfed by the pea soup fog, and tethered by a ring to a sailor at sea, I went back to Connecticut so I could pack for a guy I just promised my heart to.

1986

Journal entry: 1986 March 18 (age 22)

My my has it been years since I wrote in this. So much has happened in my life. And I certainly got the freedom and chance to experience life outside of Connecticut (Newtown).[37]

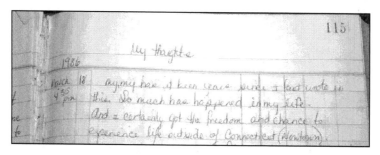

When I returned to Connecticut, I rented a bedroom from a family in Sandy Hook and secured my old job at Andrea's Bakeshop. When I called Litchfield to collect my belongings from the attic, an accusatory tone stated, "You can't come get your things."

"What do you mean, why not?"

"You took advantage of me."

"What are you talkin about? I just called you a few weeks ago, you said no problem."

He had reported all was fine, no concerns, do what I need to do. Deja vu. He sounded like my dad.

His hostility over the phone emphasized he wouldn't give me my things, so I called again. Then he claimed mice infested my belongings so he burned *everything*. I called again where he reported that *some* things were burned. His story kept changing. With this foothold of news I called on a couple of male friends to help demand the remnants of my childhood for the last time.

We rescued random boxes and aged leather suitcases and the old steam trunk I purchased with five dollars for my sixteenth birthday. A winter argyle sweater, my first jeans with patches, eight track tapes, drawings, writings, stuffed animals and other youthful tokens. What couldn't be found was a student home stereo, my sisters' wedding dress from her broken engagement, my own dowry of stainless steel bowls and a teapot, should I ever marry.

The treasures that couldn't be found, that left the biggest wake of loss, were my Brownie and Girl Scout uniforms with sparse badges sewn on its sash. Summer camp memories captured with my brownie camera; the large group camp photo and the girls I shared a cabin with. Some photos off centered or blurry. Some said it all. Others said nothing, but had been tucked into little photo corners that held their memory to the black page.

Then there was the flimsy shirt box filled with kindergarten Christmas ornaments nestled on wrinkled tissue paper faded with the past. Papier-mâché outlined the shape of a bell and Christmas stocking. They weren't perfect but rather somewhat crooked with white bumpy surfaces that held random clumps of glitter stuck in Elmer's glue. What was I going to do with these goofy little ornaments made in elementary school? It is just that they looked like something a five-year-old made and now they were gone.

I didn't know these memories represented buoys holding me up. Only when they were taken did I believe I might drown in my sorrow. Even though the loss of these silly little sentimental items held no monetary value, a piece of me became broken and lost. They represented my youth, creativity, accomplishments, dreams, or a hint of an idea. They whispered possibilities beginning and proof that a little girl had once existed.

> ...these memories represented buoys holding me up.

In the meantime the pea soup fog of 1985 had floated into 1986 while I continued to work for the next few months at the bakery, keeping my focus on moving to California to greet my sailor at the dock. Since my brother Mike was returned to Stratford, Connecticut to live with Dad, it gave me a chance to see them together. Because I was still on the good list of visits, hugs and kisses with Dad and his new wife, who claimed she loved me, I was unaware of the new nightmare my brother had been thrown back into. On any given visit, if he ever sent an S.O.S. I never noticed.

So when Dad asked me to meet him and his wife at Morrow's restaurant in Newtown, I was happy, kind of excited actually. They wanted to talk about some concerns they were having with Mike and get my two-cents. We each ordered a drink and stood at the bar side of this local establishment. I rested my elbows on the brown counter and fiddled with my cold drink sitting on the bar napkin.

As we settled in they asked how my plans were coming along to meet my sailor. "Oh great, I'm almost packed, saving money and making a banner to wave his ship in!"

Curious what they wanted to talk about I asked, "So what's going on?"

They looked me straight in the eyes and sought my advice, view, and input. How far I'd come from my childhood days of insignificance.

"Your brother's mood is changing and his grades dropped below an A."

"Really? When'd that start?"

"Since he moved back here. He came with good grades."

"So what do you think's going on?"

"We're not sure. We think maybe it's something he's eating."

The level of expertise I contributed was, "What about sugar? Are you taking him to a doctor?"

"Yah, actually this week, we have an appointment."

"Oh good, let me know what ya find out."

"Yep, once we get the results we'll call."

We hugged and kissed goodbye.

A week later at work, I received a call at the bakery from Mom in California. I heard panic in her voice. "Tam, Michael's been taken away!"

"What do you mean, taken away?" as I brushed bangs out of my face with the back of my wrist, then wiped my floured hands on my dirty apron.

"When he stepped off the school bus today, your dad and his wife wouldn't let him in the house."

"Huh? What are you talking about?"

Mom sounded defeated, "They had his belongings waiting for him in garbage bags on the porch. When he got off the bus, they told him to grab his things and load 'em up in the car. Then took him to a halfway house."

"What's a halfway house?"

"A state run institution. I don't know what's going on."

Bewildered, I wondered if this place was half-way between home and hell. I was in Connecticut trying to make sense of my life. My sister had moved to California to mend her wounds. I wanted to scream *leave me alone and let me be, I'm only 22 and at work for god's sake!* But instead I assured her I'd call Dad and find out what's going on.

Seven days ago Dad and his wife hugged me, smiled, laughed and we even shared a drink. I recounted the conversation over and over in my head. I swear they promised to call with the doctor results. What happened?

Mind game?

Maybe I heard wrong?

Not again.

Mom, across country, couldn't know all the details. There must be a mistake.

I called Dad confident I'd learn what I was sure Mom left out. Isn't this temporary? A mistake? What about the doctor? Tests? Results?

His wife answered the phone with a tone that indicated she wasn't the same person I met at Morrow's a week ago. Abrupt and closed up she said, "Let me get John for you."

When Dad came to the phone he said, "Yep."

"Uh, mom just called me at work. Something about Mike living somewhere else. Is everything okay?"

A switch in my dad had gone off. Through the phone I was met with an all too familiar silence, the kind of silence that absorbs you before you begin to sink in cold suffocating quick sand. Even over the phone my heart started to quicken as my chest was being compressed. Once again I was in the presence of my enemy.

I didn't need to see his face to sense the cold stare of his eyes boring a hole in my heart as he disconnected from all that was near to him.

Sensing his clenched teeth and even set jaw through the handset, I was met with emotionless one word syllables.

Yep.

Nope.

Bye.

He had no intention of wanting his son back and no intention of sharing with me what transpired. Not even a seething hint.

The cold distant reaction I received from Dad was as if I had betrayed him. Like my brother, I too had been dismissed by the wave of his silent hand through the phone. Our new-found relationship of the last two years dissolved with his chill.

Now that was the dad I was familiar with!

When Dad and his wife became concerned about my brother's temperament and dropping grades, an enlightened view might have been to realize this young boy was exposed to abuse, in a broken home, separated from his sisters, and sent back and forth between his conflicted parents. I imagine at one time that my brother must have wondered what was wrong with him. If that ever occurred to my parents, I never heard their concern.

I did, however, work with Mom long distance as she jumped through hoops to get Mike out. Once the legal logistics were satisfied, I collected Mike from the halfway house and he stayed with me at my one-room rental before being flown back to California. When I called Mom to let her know he was safe and with me she said, "It's ironic how when your father and I were married, he vowed that no child of his would ever be a ward of the state."

Once my brother arrived to the west coast, I continued to sock away money that I earned from the bakery so I could fly out and greet my hopeful-fiancé in California. Although Dad had stopped talking to me, I made random calls to remind him I'd be gone soon and suggested he could visit me at work. His aloof response, "That's nice." To make matters worse, a local pub he frequented, The White Birch Inn, was right across the street from the bakery where I worked.

The store front of the bakery had a full view glass window. On any given day, I could spot Dad's car parked at this local watering hole. I sold customers' morning coffee as he was getting his sun-up booze. Not only would I see his car regularly, but also Francheska, the bar's mascot, running around in the parking lot. Dad missed opportunity after opportunity to walk across the street and say hello.

Tears pooled in my eyes as I stared through the big glass window reflecting on the years of loss and the pain of his rejection. My vision blurred as I watched my dog run around in the dirt parking lot. Using my soiled white apron, I wiped tear after tear after tear until the hurt dried up. Then, with a stiff upper lip, I continued to fold pastry boxes and get our customers their morning coffee.

On Father's Day weekend 1986, I visited Aunt Dee and Uncle Joe at their home in Fairfield. Surrounded by tender love and prayers in their kitchen, I called Dad one

last time to remind him I was leaving in a couple of days to see my siblings, his kids, and hopefully his future son-in-law. I had hoped the finality of my move would instill a desire in him to want to see me one more time. With a steady, cold, unemotional tone, mixed with a hint of disdain, his final words to me were, "Have a nice life."

I met my sailor, we married and two years later divorced. It seemed neither of us knew how to unpack the baggage from our past so that we could talk about what was on our hearts. Crushed, I was unsure what a nice life should look like.

1970 Father's Day Card

Cover: Dear Father's Day?

Inside: For Daddy,
I love you very much.
Thank you for all you
do for me.
Love Tammy

TWENTY-THREE

The Hollywood Call

1991 - 1992

The call has many layers. The dreaded call. The one Hollywood movies are made of. The call which we've either experienced, heard about, or at least thought about. The call that comes after a relationship disintegrated. A relationship you thought you no longer thought about until the phone rings.

Can I ever speak to that person again?
Can I forgive them?
How will I respond?
Why should I?
Will I care?
What if I don't?

Towards the end of 1991, the phone in my Dodgington, CT apartment rang. Uncle Gene, my dad's only brother called me for the first time in my life. He called to inform me that my Dad was in the hospital fighting bone cancer, should I want to visit. This wasn't like the movies, it was real. I couldn't take another rejection. I mean, six years earlier Dad dismissed me with, "Have a nice life." Since then, my question became, "Now what?"

Journal entry: January 22, 1992 (age 28)

"Dear Lord, I'm going to try this approach for praying. I don't do well the other way, although I do talk a lot out loud maybe that's praying too. I feel it is, even when I'm upset. This is hard for me but I pray for my dad. I'm not sure what for exactly, you know how I feel about the man. I've gone from hating him to feeling sorry for him, but he still makes me angry. I pray that maybe he'll soften someday and realize he's got three great kids instead of continuing to push us away."[38]

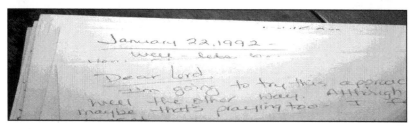

Journal entry: January 28, 1992 (age 28)

"I ran into my Uncle Gene last night, my dad's brother. He didn't have much to say, but we're not really close. I asked him how my dad was. He said, 'Okay, he goes to the hospital for treatment of his bone cancer.' I said, 'Tell him I said hi, if you see him.'"[39]

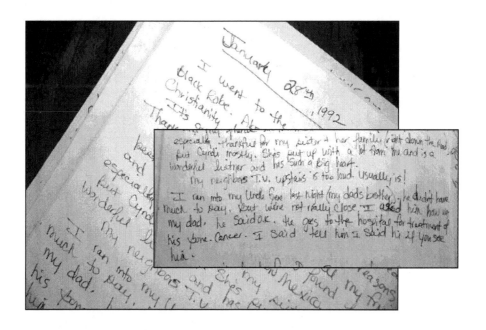

Once I informed my family about the news so they could make their own choices about how to handle Uncle Gene's call, I stewed on the choice set before me.

My childhood was filled with verbal, physical and emotional abuse. The past six years were filled with silence, no visits, calls or cards from Dad. Would going to the hospital piece together all that was tattered?

If I walk into his hospital room will sunshine beams stream through the vertical blinds of the institutional window near his bedside? Will harmonious music fill the pensive air as I'm genuinely embraced by my dad? Will he hug me while whispering, "I'm sorry honey." Will tears stream down our faces cleansing years of meanness and ugliness from our hearts? Will his hand gently brush away these tears from my cheeks as he tells me I am his little princess after all and that he has always loved me?

What daughter wouldn't want this chance for repair? Why would I delay visiting my dad in the hospital? My willing spirit asked what if this is the last opportunity? Isn't the death bed where healing takes place? Maybe he would show remorse or regret or say he's sorry. Maybe he would say he's missed his kids and loves us or maybe he would just be glad we came. It's possible he would show a small effort to impart a father's blessing that would help repair and move us forward in life. Maybe he would get emotional in a tender sort of way. At least squeak out something to show he cared.

But then my willing spirit paused as my protective guard asked, *why would I go at all, let alone run to his bedside? Do I have the resiliency left in my reservoir to be dismissed again?*

February 1992

Many of my questions were answered in a simple unexpected way when my sister went back into that arena one more time. A few years earlier she had returned from California to settle in Connecticut, married with her husband Bill, a wonderful man who adores her. So after they learned about *the call*, they made several attempts in January to visit Dad in the hospital, but circumstances on both ends thwarted their efforts. Finally in February of 1992, they connected by phone. When Dad answered the phone he welcomed C.J., meaning he was civil and did not hang up on her.

At first my sister's exchange was polite. However, a word, phrase or tone triggered Dad. He turned on a dime and their conversation took a nose dive.

By the end of the call with my sister, Dad unabashedly imparted his final blessing ...

"None of you kids respected me or my wife. As a matter of fact all three of you kids are no good and stupid, and you can all go to hell. And by the way, tell your sister her fuckin' dog is dead."

I no longer had any doubts whether or not I would visit or call my dad in the hospital.

TWENTY-FOUR

One Tiny Paragraph

Imet a great guy in June of 1992 at a country western music bar in Connecticut. After an intelligent conversation and a few dances later, we exchanged phone numbers.

A month later, and after many phone conversations, my new boyfriend, Curtis, visited me at my apartment in Newtown. It was a charming two-room unit inside an old farmhouse. While I made him a cold drink to quench the July heat, I reported about an unexpected call I'd received from my aunt.

Aunt Dee, my mother's sister, who is always generous with her time and conversation on the phone, struggled uncharacteristically with her choice of words when I answered her call.

"Are you okay, Tam?"

"Yeah, why do you ask?"

"Has anything happened that you forgot to tell me?"

"Uh, not that I can think of, did I miss an event or something?"

She hesitated before imparting her awkward news bulletin on me.

"I ran into your Aunt Bev the other day while I was out running errands. We had an interesting conversation that I need to share with you."

"Okay, you've got my attention now."

"Bev surprised me when she said, 'I'm sorry about the loss.' But I didn't know what she was referring to so of course I asked what loss? Tam, she told me your dad died."

Silence. Then, "My dad's dead?"

"So you didn't know Tam?"

"No, this is the first time I'm hearing this. Wow! Do you know when he died?"

"Bev said he died four months ago on March 17."

As Aunt Dee unfolded the news, I now understood her gentle verbal fishing when I first answered the phone. It became clear why she thought I forgot to tell her something because how could I not know my dad died, let alone four months ago. But I didn't.

As I recounted the call in a businesslike manner to Curtis, he said, "Considering the heft of the news, you sound pretty detached."

"I do? I'm just tellin' you what happened."

If I had any hopes of keeping this guy around long enough to learn about me, describing what could appear as detrimental baggage wasn't exactly dating material. Where would I begin to explain to this man, by all rights a stranger, why I may appear aloof? Would I start with the last time Dad and I talked? Blame it on the booze? Their divorce or what led to the divorce? Perhaps I appeared indifferent because Dad pushed me away most of my life and his final exclamation point, large and bold, shut me out of the last six years of his life. How should one respond to the news and what should it feel like?

By the fall of 1992 my family wondered why Dad's wife never called to tell us he died so C.J. called our dad's widow and inquired. Without blinking an eye over the phone, she charged, "You kids didn't deserve to know because you never called your dad or loved him."

What a joke She had to be kidding. I was furious when my sister told me what she said. Who did she think she was? How dare she take away our right to choose and decide how we might want closure with our dad? Of course I know he was no angel but after she married my dad I found it interesting that he changed his mind about giving me back my dog and as their drinking increased, they gave away my brother. So I ask you, "Is it detached or survival or numbness or just the way life is?"

Soon after receiving my sister's report, I contacted the widow who was willing to let me visit. Thank God Curtis was still hanging around and welcomed the adventure.

Breaking the ice in her living room I asked, "Will there be a service?"

"A memorial of some kind, but eventually his ashes will be scattered at sea."

"What's the date of the service?"

"I don't know," she stammered. "I'll let you know when I know something." Her tone and body language showed no signs of regret or a willingness to care. It was as if my presence irritated her conscience.

Perhaps warped, but I still wanted some connection to my dad. An instrument, photo, something, anything. I asked about his guitar or banjo. These weren't heirlooms but gifts that Mom purchased for him back in the 70s. The widow's curt response was, "I have nothing to give you and no, there aren't any instruments here." My request for anything of Dad's frustrated her. Our visit went from civil to short to over.

Later I contacted vital statistics and obtained a copy of Dad's obituary.

A tiny paragraph with few words reflected the sadness of his life.

The obituary listed one child; "a loving son and daughter-in-law."

But Dad has three kids!

And our brother wasn't married.

Who were these people?

Probing inquiries proved it wasn't a typo.

They were neighbors who loved our dad like a dad and he loved them as his own.

We'll never know if the words chosen for Dad's obituary were his wishes, his wife's, or theirs as a couple.

What I do know is one tiny paragraph revealed we didn't exist in our father's eyes.

An opportunity for love, forgiveness, remorse, repair.

Instead, one last act of meanness to the grave.

One tiny paragraph.

His final act of rejection in black and white.

TWENTY-FIVE

So Who Do I Blame?

Noah Webster 1828 American Dictionary defines BLAME: 1. To censure; to express disapprobation of; to find fault with; opposed to praise or commend, and applicable most properly to persons, but applied also to things. I must blame your conduct; or I must blame you for neglecting business. 2. To bring reproach upon; to blemish; to injure. She had blamed her noble blood.[40]

After Dad beat into me the message *life is tough*, along with eighteen years of physical, verbal and emotional abuse, I was prepared to face the world where it really must be tough out there. My first eighteen years offered mixed messages which produced confusion of identity, lack of confidence, and stupid choices thanks to a faulty navigating system where I stumbled into my adult life with clumsy fashion. I felt cheated of the fairy-tale childhood one might hope to have.

So who do I blame? According to Mom, she had a classic Vermont childhood woven with idyllic memories of innocence and loving stable parents, an upbringing right out of a Norman Rockwell painting. She recalled picturesque playful scenes from summer days when she and her sister Dee, had active imaginations and their homemade map led them to hidden treasures. They galloped on the log in the woods, rode bikes, dodged inchworms hanging from trees, played make-believe with whatever the game of the day was. Their local community

175

center housed the bowling alley, which still had pin boys on the first floor and the roller skating rink was on the second.

Aunt Cookie, a Fresh Air Child from New York City, visited Mom's family one summer in 1946 and the rest is history. She came to Vermont every summer from then on and became part of our family. Mom, Cookie and Dee became fast friends and sisters as they put on summer plays and fought over whose turn it was to sleep on the crack between the twin beds. Cookie called my grandparents Mommy and Daddy and they loved her as if she was their own flesh and blood. The family harmony allowed their innocent girlish ways to bud and blossom in a carefree manner unfettered from fear of their home front. So how did my youth miss this DNA?

My mother started out with promise and dreams like any young woman looking for love. In her day the legal age for marriage was twenty-one so should she want to marry earlier, she'd have to get her parent's blessing. By age twenty she considered herself an old maid and passed by because her parents and sister had married by nineteen.

By the time my parents met and set their wedding date Mom turned the legal age just in the nick of time. However, she still hoped to receive their blessing because they were divided over their daughter marrying a man with a serious health issue. Because of Dad's life expectancy, grandmother was concerned about their future so she held back her blessing. My grandfather told Mom, if she loved him, marry him and be happy for whatever time you have. Therefore, she married him.

So who do I blame? Do I blame her for not knowing better? Yet, know better about what? Did the era make her believe she was a spinster? Or was it because of her era that she truly had a delightful childhood and her innocence assumed it would carry into her marriage forever and ever? Do I blame my mother's girlish dreams and her naiveté? But aren't we all naïve until we aren't? Perhaps my mother had a big heart and thought she could nurse this man, through sickness and through health. Or like all young love, had she no idea the responsibility she committed to when she said, "I do?" Should I blame my maternal grandparents for Mom's thinking which must have come from them, or did it? On the other hand, what was wrong with Mom's thinking, anything? We all dream and hope.

Is it possible she was clinging to the unspoiled hopefulness of her childhood? Perhaps she remained optimistic about her dreams and the promises of her wedding vows. So then why wouldn't she have believed her husband each time he said, "I will change and this time it will be different?"

So who do I blame? My father was young once and started out with promise. A little towhead born during the depression, his upbringing was far from a Norman Rockwell painting. If anything, his painting more resembled the Scream.

The front page of the Bridgeport, Connecticut Times-Star newspaper, dated January 7, 1938, reads "Disease of Kings Hits Baby." [41]

A reporter came to my dad's house to write about the "Rare Malady" in his article titled, Disease of Kings Hits Baby. He reported that within the week after Christmas, my dad, only two years old, cut his lip on a new toy. The cut wouldn't stop bleeding for days.

Ironically, hemophilia has been called the "Royal Disease."[42] I never received the royal princess treatment, nor walked down the red carpet. I rather suspect my dad wondered where his royal crown was and highly doubt he felt like he had royal blood in him. This was probably more like a royal pain in his butt!

Johnny Peterson, 2 1-2 years, husky son of a West End WPA workman is shown above with his sister Julia or "Nooky", as he calls her. Despite his apparent health, John is afflicted with that rare blood disorder haemophilia.

Rare Malady Menaces Life Of WPA Worker's Baby Son

Haemophilia, Bane of Spanish Royalty, Strikes at Modest Family Here—Infant, Husky Despite Ailment, Laughs on Way to Hospital

BY EDWARD J. DENNEHY

Haemophilia—the blood-letting disease that has been the bane of Spanish royalty, today cast its dread shadow over the life of...

Rare Malady Menaces Life Of WPA Worker's Baby Son

Haemophilia, Bane of Spanish Royalty, Strikes at Modest Family Here—Infant, Husky Despite Ailment, Laughs on Way to Hospital

BY EDWARD J. DENNEHY

Haemophilia—the blood-letting disease that has been the bane of Spanish royalty—today cast its dread shadow over the life of a two-and-one-half year old husky Bridgeport baby boy, the son of a poverty-stricken WPA workman. The boy is blond Johnny Peterson, who resides in a small back-hall flat of a tenement house at 591 Bostwick Ave., with his parents and three brothers and sisters.

Johnny, a well-knit lad bubbling with cheerfulness and general good health, is the victim of this hereditary trouble. According to Bridgeport hospital officials, his is the first case of this type that institution has handled. The boy's maternal grandfather and maternal uncle died at an early age from this trouble.

Johnny was playing earlier this week with the few toys that Santa Claus had brought him for Christmas when suddenly he cut his lower lip slightly. On Tuesday the wound began to bleed profusely. The blood-letting has continued almost unceasingly since. Mrs. Peterson took the boy to the Emergency hospital yesterday. He was treated there by Dr. D. W. Pasquariello who gave the mother a pass to Bridgeport hospital for further treatment.

The flow of blood failed to stop and the worried mother was again prepared to take her baby to Bridgeport hospital this morning when a Times-Star reporter arrived at the modest Peterson flat.

GOING "BYE-BYE"

GOING "BYE-BYE"

Mrs. Peterson had just given her children their breakfast at 9 a. m. when the newspaperman entered. Johnny, smiling and happy because he was going "bye-bye" was bundled up in a warm navy blue jacket and leggings. Despite a certain paleness because of the loss of blood, Johnny showed no other effects of haemophilia. He was not a bit frightened when the Times-Star cameraman posed him in a parlor chair with his four-year-old sister Julia for a picture. He snuggled up close to "Nooky," as he calls her, and gave a big smile to the camera.

Mrs. Peterson accepted the offer of a ride to Bridgeport hospital. The reporter picked the husky lad

Concluded on Page Two

RARE MALADY

Continued from Page One
up to carry him down stairs. As he did so, Johnny gurgled deceivingly. He uncorked a vicious right that landed on the back of the writer's head and almost spelled disaster for the newsman's glasses.

Mrs. Mae Arone, a neighbor who was going to mind the other children while Mrs. Peterson and Johnny were away, jokingly warned, Johnny, "You won't go bye-bye if you aren't a good boy."

"Oh, I'm a good boy," the baby decided and the trip down from the third floor was marked by friendly relations between the writer and the high-spirited baby.

ON MOTHER'S SIDE

Mrs. Peterson revealed that about a year ago Johnny had a slight attack of the disease when he cut himself for the first time. When his case was then diagnosed as haemophilia, Mrs. Peterson realized fully that the baby was subject to the trouble that caused her father and brother to die at an early age.

The mother, of course, is greatly

worried. "I don't mind when the children are sick from common illnesses. But when Johnny's sick from something like this—oh, it's terrible. And he's such a grand little baby too."

I'll be particularly worried when he gets older and goes to school. If he falls down or gets knocked down, they won't be able to do anything for him, if he is cut badly," Mrs. Peterson said. "If he's in something like an auto accident, it will be too bad too."

Mrs. Peterson, a comparatively young mother, is devoted to Johnny.

"I hate to see him in the hospital," she remarked. "You can only see him twice a week and I get so lonesome and worried, even with the other children. When he was in the hospital the last time, I used to go up and stand outside the nursery window and try and hear if I could hear him cry. I hope he won't have to stay in the hospital again."

Haemophilia, Dr. Pasquariello explained yesterday, is hereditary and transmitted by mothers, although the mothers themselves are not affected by it. It appears only in males. Cases of it in Bridgeport have been extremely rare. The Count de Covadonga, a Spanish prince, was recently confined to a New York city hospital with the affliction.

The other Peterson children are Jacqueline, 7; Julia, 4; and Eugene.

Dad had Hemophilia Type A which consists of three levels, mild, moderate and severe.[43] Dad had severe and at the time there was no cure. The life expectancy was low and concern for his was justified because his maternal grandfather, Hans Christian Schmidt, died at age twenty-nine and his uncle died at age four. Both were hemophiliacs. The clotting factor for a Hemophiliac was in the early stages of discovery in 1937.[44]

In addition to the short straw Dad drew for hemophilia, he and his four siblings were taken from their mother due to neglectful child rearing and placed into the foster care system. Other than Grandma Laura being a lousy housekeeper and labeled as an unfit mother, I have yet to learn what the real story of neglect was. Perhaps when her husband, Mr. Peterson, died in 1942, being a single mom wasn't easy. The word was, my dad, who was seven at the time of Mr. Peterson's death, didn't really know him.

I had learned that foster homes were uncomfortable taking Dad because they were unsure how to handle a sick child with the magnitude of his needs. Therefore, he was passed from one home to another. One foster home put him in a covered crib even though he was well past crib age. He shared with my mom that he would try to escape that crib as if it was a prison cell. In the 1930s and 1940s, the lack of knowledge and proper medicine made it hard to embrace a little sick boy with bleeding issues. In those days before factor VIII, he would have had to be driven to the nearest hospital for a blood transfusion, if he was brought at all. A visible cut on the outside of his body was obvious, but internal bleeding was not. Often he would not know he had internal bleeding until he woke with a bruise or stiff joints the next morning.

Playing and falling as all children do created risk for permanent joint damage. In fact at age five, when Dad  lived at a state-run institution for sick children, he fell off the swing and injured his knee. He was sent to bed with an ice pack but his knee never healed properly so he walked with a limp the remainder of his life.

In the meantime Dad's four siblings were all placed in the home of the, Gratto's, a house painter and his wife, where they remained until they were grown. Eventually Dad was placed there too, but he would run away several times to be with his biological mother. He wouldn't have understood why he was taken from her, he just wanted his mom. What little boy doesn't hope his mother would see him as a young man with much potential? After frequent attempts, to be with her, at age 10 he ran away and continued to live with her for two more years until her second husband, Victor Sovereign, died May 7, 1950 at which time Dad was sent away to live in other foster homes.

Dad's mother, Laura Emma Schmidt Sovereign from Bridgeport, Connecticut, had an older sister Marie Hanson who lived in Denmark. Below are two excerpts from letters written by Marie to her younger sister Laura Emma, nine years after the rare malady article had been written about Dad. We were privileged to have these letters translated from Danish to English.

Esbjerg, Danmark December 16, 1947

My Dear Sister!

Yes, now I will write (to) you, dear sister, and I hope you will get it for Christmas. I have, as you know, not heard from you, since I wrote the last time. I mailed a letter to you the 21 of October, and hope you got it. I hope you all are well. How is your little boy? I have myself tried a lot of sickness I know what it is. I can tell you that our daughter is in the hospital...[45]

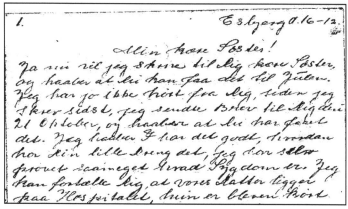

Esbjerg, Danmark January 21, 1948

Dear sister Laura Emma,

Yes, now I believe it is about time to get the pen going again, it is long since I got your letter for my birthday. I guess, you did not understand, why it took so long. I do not understand how time runs away (from one) one has far too much to do. Time does not suffice. And I believe you must have it somewhat alike, as you write, you must go out for work, that has not been easy for you, I presume. After you have had two small boys to take care of, and so much sickness to battle with, it is difficult, I have tried it myself. But it appears to me, that as you have your husband now, you don't write what he is doing. In case he has a good job, it should be possible for you to stay home with the children. You did not write anything about when you lost *your first husband and what he died of.*[46]

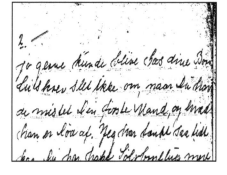

As a youth, Dad was seen around the streets on the west side of Bridgeport pushing himself face down in a red wagon when his legs wouldn't work for him. Joe, Dad's future brother-in-law, was one of the kids in the streets of Bridgeport during the 1940s who remembered seeing the boy in the wagon.

During the times Dad couldn't walk but wanted to go to Long Island beach he rode his bike. The story goes; he'd crawl to his bike, climb on and pedal to the beach, get off and crawl into the water to swim. He'd been told a couple of times by doctors he'd never walk again, but he proved them wrong.

Tutors came to Dad's home because he missed much public schooling due to his hemophilia. When he made it to the seventh grade he was sixteen and taller than all his classmates' so he decided he was done with school.

During the Korean War in 1951 Dad turned sixteen so he was required to sign up for the draft. When he went to obtain his birth certificate at the registrar's office he was informed they had no record of a John Peterson. He made a new discovery about himself that day when he learned his real name was Gioacchino Peterson, not John. He also learned that he was named after a man he never met, Gioacchino Giuliano. Had Dad been given his surname, he would have been known as Gioacchino Giuliano junior. This revealed that his father, Mr. Peterson, was not his biological father. It also shed light on why it seemed he loathed his mother later in life.

Upon turning eighteen, he received a letter stating he'd have to sign up for the military. Because he was a hemophiliac, he knew he'd receive a 4F classification. However, in an effort to follow the process, the story goes something like this; his first attempt to go was delayed because he was laid up from hemorrhaging (internal bleeding) and during the second attempt, his car broke down on the way to the draft board. He decided instead to go to Pennsylvania with a friend and sell magazines door-to-door. In the meantime, one of his sister's back in Connecticut tried to locate him because he was considered a draft dodger and now on the FBI's wanted list. When he returned from selling magazines, he went straight to the draft board where they declared him 4F. The Military Classification of 4F is not qualified for military service due to medical reasons,[47] while other commentaries and definitions implied people with a 4F were considered failures, not only for the military but the dating population.[48]

When Dad learned his identity was not his and became classified as unfit to serve his country, I wonder if it added salt to his wound of life and death health issues and foster homes. God only knows what seeds were being planted in his fiber about his worth and value.

Someone once told Dad that Gioacchino meant King so at times he would call himself John King Peterson. How peculiar that he was referred to as the baby with the King's disease. His mother's foolhardy affair left him with a mystery. What was that person's genetic line? Where was his father? Did he leave him a blessing? To say the least, my dad didn't appear to have a sweet start to life. When he told me it was his job to toughen me up, maybe that was the best advice he could muster and maybe that was my father's blessing to me. No wonder I resonated with the song, "A Boy Named Sue."

So who do I blame, the royal disease or Grandma Laura, for passing it onto my dad?

Do I blame the father my dad never knew, or the man he thought was his father? Where was his parental guidance?

In 1901 Grandma Laura was two months old when her father Hans Christian Schmidt died. Maybe that's why she looked for love in all the wrong places. Maybe she was looking to be that princess in someone's eyes too. So who would she blame?

Whose fault was all of this? Did the death of my sister spur on Dad's anger?

Did the crash of the building boom cause our family angst? Where were family relatives? Didn't anybody see? Was it ever their job to see?

If we all come from the same family culture, why would we think there's a problem?

So who do I blame? I found varying versions of Edvard Munch's poem on his painting, Scream. One rendition reads: *I was walking along a path with two friends – the sun was setting – suddenly the sky turned blood red – I paused, feeling exhausted, and leaned on the fence – there was blood and tongues of fire above the blue-black fjord and the city – my friends walked on, and I stood there trembling with anxiety – and I sensed an infinite scream passing through nature.*[49]

For all the ranting and raving my dad rained on our family, I wondered if he ever got to release his scream.

My quest has been to find a cause for all the pain and loss I suffered. There had to be a reason this happened. It cannot be senseless or I fear my existence is in vain. Someone must be at fault for the hostility I received.

So who pays the bill for this mess? In my ongoing pursuit to break the cycle of brokenness, I discovered I didn't have to dig far beneath the surface of my history to reveal bits and pieces of human frailty which began to get in the way of my determined hunt for blame.

My search was no longer a straight shot as I began to uncover innocence, vulnerability and delicate layers of brokenness which seemed to have been present long before I ever existed.

> ...pieces of human frailty began to get in the way of my determined hunt for blame.

In the end, who do I point a finger at when everything started somewhere, and when that somewhere made sense to someone, Once Upon A Time....

TWENTY-SIX

The Fragile Dance

1992

Who are we kidding? When boy meets girl, boy wants sex and girl wants to feel loved. Perhaps they are desperately seeking true love, but deep inside they don't want to appear desperate so instead, they share a fake part of themselves to avoid feeling vulnerable.

We're like little seeds whose hardy fragile pods require care. If scattered in the breeze, our fate may be stepped on, drowned, or burned in the sun or eaten by birds. If seeds aren't cultivated in fertile soil, they risk being neglected and wasted.[50]

However, in spite of the carelessness, some seeds will land between crags filled with a pittance of soil. They'll burrow, cling, reach for the sun and be refreshed with the rain. They are determined to become the creation that was put inside their little shell. If allowed proper space, their buds will bloom and share their rich fragrant color. That is of course if they aren't eaten by a woodchuck.

Maybe the boy and girl are like a flower garden in need of fresh seeds and fresh soil because over time their garden bed had been neglected and poisoned; so weeds need to be pulled, stalks pruned, and old gnarly roots that have hindered their growth need to be cut away.[51] And when the infatuation wears off and they have discovered that they both want the same thing; to be noticed, respected and appreciated, to have a companion to help, someone to have fun and grow old with when no one else will have them,

perhaps they ask, *now what do we do so we don't get hurt
again?*

The dance of the decision to take a risk is
challenging enough when our seed is fostered in a home
that seems to have it all together. When it isn't, sometimes
it's hard to know the difference between making stupid or
wise decisions. This is when we dance with two left feet and
it becomes all the more hard to believe, trust, and give of
ourselves. The moment of these choices becomes fragile.

Who says Prince Charming has to come on a white
horse and kiss me awake to a better life? Sure, a princess
dress looks pretty but I'm not a fan of bras, never mind
corsets. Jeans with patches, bare feet and daisies in my
hair are more my speed.

So rather than lying in a sunny field of wild flowers
day dreaming and waiting to be rescued by a kiss, I sat
alone at a table for six in a dimly-lit room which failed to
appear romantic. It was more like a dungeon of souls
hoping to find Mr. or Mrs. Right, but ready to go home with
Mr. or Mrs. Tonight. Divorced three years and meeting Mr.
Wrong every time I turned around, I was fed up with men
and empty promises. The only reason I had been at this
joint was to support my sister C.J. and brother-in-law Bill's
fifth wedding anniversary.

They wanted to cheer with an evening of two-steppin'
and shooting pool. Finding local bands that played country
music in Connecticut during the 90s wasn't as difficult as
finding a venue with a dance floor larger than two tables
put together, but we did.

He didn't ride in on a horse, but rather buzzed like a
bee to honey as he made his way across the dance hall and

asked, "Is this seat taken? Can I join you?" The day I met my future, I was wearing a blue calico skirt with a white eyelet top and Tony Lama cowgirl boots from El Paso, Texas. He was wearing tight jeans, cowboy boots and over his shirt was a purple denim jacket with the sleeves cut off. His white Stetson cowboy hat, from Salt Lake City, Utah, slightly revealed his long sandy blonde curls pulled back in a ponytail while his most adorable frame revealed a healthy fit male who bench pressed at the gym. Nothing about him was shy but his demeanor was polite and courteous while his bright blue eyes made life seem possible.

As the fifth wheel of the group, I'd been sitting alone at least twenty minutes to save our table while the other two couples shot pool. Somewhat intrigued that a man came to life and wanted to talk to me, I assessed the situation and deemed he looked harmless enough so I granted him permission to join me. This man, my future husband, a seasoned musician, was there scoping out the club to book a gig, not a wife. I, his future wife, was there to support her family, not interested in making stupid small talk.

Reserved and not impressed at this time of life with the male species, here we were anyway as we managed small talk across the table from one another. The loud music forced me to stand and lean over the table to hear him. Each time I leaned, my hand held the scoop neckline of my shirt so he wouldn't get the impression I was inviting him in.

It occurred to me this guy wasn't throwing me one line clichés but rather stringing complete thoughts and sentences together. I became hopeful as he redeemed for me that a man and woman could have an intelligent conversation. By the time I relaxed and let my guard down I felt a hand on my shoulder. I turned and looked up to find my brother-in-law Bill behind me. He wasted no time, looked right at this man Curtis and said, "Why are you talking to my wife?"

Can I tell you, if looks could kill, Bill would be dead and buried ten feet under snapdragons! I mean, seriously, here was the first real guy who approached me all night. And he even knew how to talk talk. They stared across the table at each other while Bill stood his ground behind me. Curtis never flinched during the silent interrogation. Then all of a sudden both revealed a glimmer in their eyes and they started laughing like two long lost buddies. Here were two men who had a code only they understood. I had no idea what transpired, but whatever the secret man-code was it didn't scare Curtis away. Instead, they looked at each other, smiled, shook hands and the rest, as they say, is history. I don't claim to speak man-code but today I know this, Bill cared enough to challenge this stranger and protect me.

Finally, Curtis asked me to dance. Gene Kelly and Debbie Reynolds we weren't. Well, how could we be when as fast as he'd pull me close to his chest, I'd push him away at arm's length. Let's just say we weren't going to win any awards. Curtis will share: "Every time she pushed me away I knew she was the girl for me!"

When the evening ended, he asked for my phone number. How original. Well, I decided he appeared safe enough so I gave it to him. How typical. But truth be known when he told me he lived an hour from me I was certain no matter how nice he seemed, I'd never hear from this man again. Surprise, surprise. The next day he called and the following weekend he drove his beat-up old green van down to Newtown. We met at the commuter parking lot off exit eleven. As the days and weeks followed, he continued driving down to see me. We discovered we were attracted to one another because the varying wounds of our past gave us a language that understood the different shades of our hurts. We also learned that we both enjoyed the outdoors so we hiked and explored as we became acquainted.

After about a month of dating Curtis, I planned a homemade dinner of beef stroganoff and to set the mood, I put a Merle Haggard album on my record player. Divine intervention was sowing seeds in what would soon be our new garden. When he arrived and stepped into my farmhouse apartment, he stopped in his tracks. Unbeknownst to me, I'd made one of his favorite meals and put his all-time favorite artist on my turntable.

Our encounter was not storybook fairy tale style. We both came into our union, fragile and scattered. Uncertain and untrusting. Yearning and hopeful, but skeptical. The hurts and trials we both carried in our shells were reason enough to hesitate before letting our guard down to take a risk. The proverbial baggage we each carried came loaded with years of broken tools, confusion and heartbreak. He also came from a broken marriage.

The invisible signs we wore flashed like neon lights in a bar room window.

Me, a survivor of abuse.
My dad, an abusive alcoholic.
My future husband, a recovered alcoholic.

Illustration: Why is everyone I meet an alcoholic?

We tried hard to hide from our past hurts yet the irony of the wound is it drew us like a magnet to the only thing familiar to us. Similar sorrows unwittingly attracted us to the kind of person we tried to run away from, the culture of ourselves.

> Similar sorrows unwittingly attracted us to the kind of person we tried to run away from.

But rather than hold each other hostage with fingers that point, blame, and perpetuate our pasts, we took a risk in hope, that we'd be willing to grow together to overcome our wounds with victory.

I wasn't asleep in that perfect sunny field wearing a beautiful princess dress and my lips didn't glisten glossy red waiting for that kiss. He didn't come wearing a coat of armor while charging on a white horse and he had no sword in a sheath to rescue me from the dragon.

In spite of following some wrong road signs, we found each other with broken hearts, bruised egos, fractured thoughts and a willingness to try again. Why? Because there is always hope. We believed in new beginnings and wanted to become awake and alive in new ways.

> Why? Because there is always hope.

There were no magic wands or little fairies buzzing about sprinkling fairy dust while floating cupids played the magic harp. But we had Merle Haggard and a good steak after a hardy hike. The singer songwriter in my soon-to-be-husband came alive in new ways as we healed from old relationships while growing together anew.

Inspired, he wrote our wedding song, 'I Stand Before You.'
I stand before you, with all of my reason
With one act of treason, my heart gave in to you

You stand before me, in all of your beauty
Accepting the duty, of life lived hand in hand
You stand before me, I stand before you

We stand before them, cause seeing's believing
And now we are leaving, the lonely we used to be

I know love can break, but ours will stand the strain
Into the darkest night the light shines through again ...[52]
Excerpt from "I Stand Before You" by Curtis Willey c.1996

We were planted in new soil and given another shot at it. And with the best of what we had to offer each other, we believed in our Gardner while the question begged, *As I stand before you, will you dance the fragile dance with me?*

Perhaps after all, my story is a fairy tale come true.

TWENTY-SEVEN

The Gift

January - March 2004

Traveling two hundred and sixty-one miles towards Route 89 north took a little over four hours to our destination, St. Albans, Vermont. Me and my mother, in a car for four hours and sixteen minutes to be exact. In January 2004, Mom had flown in from California so I could drive her to Vermont to attend her favorite aunt's funeral. I loved my great Aunt Regie and her late husband Uncle Jerry.

During my childhood, Mom drove us to their home numerous times. Their house was almost to the Canadian border. As a little girl, I thought it took forever to get to White River Junction where our great grandmother lived, so when we drove to St. Albans it seemed we'd never arrive.

Aunt Regie would open the porch door with a calm nod as if we'd walked in from down the street, her Vermont accent welcoming us in, "Wahl hello thare. Come ahn in. Jus' put ya things up stayars." As a child, I was fascinated to watch her mouth speak. The ayuh that would come out of her mouth, hardly a twitch of her lips, made her look like a ventriloquist as her eyes sparkled with love. Although my voice didn't sound like hers, her funny accent depicted my ancestry, reminding me of my Vermont roots.

After claiming the bed we'd sleep in, my sister and I ran downstairs and fought to see who'd be the first to land on Uncle Jerry's lap and smoke his pipe. Greeted by the wafting aroma of his tobacco, his jovial twinkle was enough to know he loved me.

At age forty, I was happy to accompany my mother during a memorable piece of her life as she said goodbye to her aunt. Because Mom moved to California twenty years earlier, it'd been quite some time since she'd  been to this neck of the woods. Although most goodbyes are hard, the funeral became a day of hellos with long ago family members.

Of course it became an event for me too. Seeing second cousins, faces and names from my adolescent years was a flashback. But no matter how much time went by, everyone remembered the year I slept over Aunt Regie and Uncle Jerry's. Many chuckled as they recalled the boy who had taken me on a date to the cow bahn up the road to his fahm. When he called the next day Aunt Regie handed me the phone, "There's a boy on the phone foiya, he wants to talk to yah." Then her and Uncle Jerry hid around the corner and held back their laugh as they watched me blush. We were smitten with each other but my fifteen-year-old hormones and I had to return to Connecticut the next day.

After sympathies, tears, smiles and regaling of old stories that seemed like yesterday, we swapped phone numbers and email addresses. Mom and I gathered our coats and bags, and then hugged our Vermont family goodbye.

We made a detour to Springfield, Vermont so Mom could reminisce. I enjoyed revisiting her old stomping grounds as she showed me around. We drove past the old community center that had a bowling alley and a roller skating rink on the second floor. She pointed to what looked like fire escape stairs on the outside of the building and remarked how as young girls they'd walked up and down with their roller skates on to get to the rink. On our way out of town, we visited the old house on Rita Street where she and Aunt Dee grew up.

Done with our mini excursion, my mother and I braced ourselves for the long drive back to Connecticut. The distance was long enough, but time like this together alone in the car was new ground. No doubt we talked and all was fine, but I mean we never seemed to talk about anything real. It was always shallow and trivial. There was always an unspoken awkwardness between us for as long as I could remember. I mean, for like a long, long, long time. Like since at least my adolescent years, if not longer.

But like everything else misunderstood, all that is unsaid between us gets written off as insolence, the weather, they're kids, bad day, broken and divorced family, dysfunctional, that was then, this is now, or bury the past and move on.

Back in Connecticut, my husband and sister and I had one last visit with Mom before sending her back home to her second husband. We settled into our living room to talk about the funeral, relatives and the visit in general. One conversation led to another and we were off and running. We let our hair down with a few laughs and reminiscent stories. In fun, Curtis asked Mom for the scoop on me as a teenager. When else does one get the opportunity to get the dirt on a loved one than when they're surrounded by the sources, their loved ones?

Without batting an eye, my mother recounted two specific events. Like a tape recorder, she depressed her pause button after twenty-plus years and hit re-play. One event was a harmless adolescent prank that resolved itself and the other was when I ran away. As she reported the specifics of my insubordinate behavior for running away, her tone revealed resentment when she emphasized how much I had made her worry. I'm not sure why, but so many years later the edge in her voice spit out the account as if it happened yesterday. And had it been yesterday? I was stunned at her disconnect. Somehow she missed some facts. Like, Dad was why I ran away. Like, I was tired of being belittled, yelled at and smacked and shoved and beat-up.

Moms lack of connection always gave me the message that I'm the one who did something wrong, not Dad. And this was no exception. This began to explain the awkward divide between us. I was forty and this old conversation exhausted me yet again. I'm certain this wasn't the can of worms my husband's innocent question intended to open, nor was it the can I was prepared for.

Because I'd heard these stories before I said to myself, *oh brother, here we go again,* but I was unable to keep my tone jovial. Years of irritation jumped right in as I barked, "And why did I run away?" Drawing my verbal line in the sand, I rebutted, "Really, how many times must we talk about this?"

Like a caged animal up against the wall, my mother retaliated, "You've always been independent as long as I can remember. In fact you intimidated me as young as five years old, don't you remember?" Her eyes grew wide as she searched my face for validation of her accusation.

Before I knew what hit me she concluded with vehement desperation, "In fact you and your intimidating personality came between me and your dad, actually, more like since you were two."

Well, there was the loudest silent thud you can imagine. Talk about coming out of left field. This put an end to the fun get-to-know-ya family repartee. I looked to my sister for a clue at what the heck happened, but she played a good poker face. I wanted to call Mom out on what was an obvious faux pas, but social etiquette stopped my mouth from letting her have it. The voice in my head said *It's not polite to call her out in front of others, she's your mother,* so instead I froze. I'm sure divine intervention also played a part and kept me from saying something I'd later regret.

After Mom boarded the plane, instead of phone calls and emails, six-silent-weeks passed while I sorted out my thoughts and implications of the parting shot she'd left with me. If I'd learned anything from elementary days, it was sound advice that suggested, if I can't find anything nice to say, then don't say anything at all.

I was the oldest which meant anything that went wrong was my fault because somehow, I was supposed to know-better. At least that was one of many messages I received growing up. So after the absurd offense was hurled, I actually contemplated what I'd done to come between my parents. The sickness within the sickness of our unhealthy family is that I found relief when Mom changed her accusation from age five to age two because my head rationalized that the younger I was, the less capable I was to have come between them.

> "The abuse from my past leaves me confused about which things I am actually responsible for in my life. This diseased view doesn't go away without effort." TSW 53

Over the years, I had chosen my battles, letting many comments go. What the heck, she's in California. However, the bomb dropped made all infractions inside me implode so that it became imperative to find release. If there was to be any resolution, truly heal, and grow in our mother-daughter relationship, it was apparent we needed to talk about more than the weather. Remaining emotionally closed to avoid confronting my mom wasn't going to serve either of us. I wasn't intent on hurting her, but evading the obvious and not shedding light on the truth was doing more damage to our relationship and our personhood.

Making small talk and pretending there was never a rift between us wasn't working anymore. The gap, more like a chasm, was wider than the three-thousand miles between Connecticut and California. What did I have to lose? If I said nothing, I'd never know if we could repair anything. The repair needed was obvious because of her statement which said, *my little two-year-old daughter and her personality came between my husband and me, the adults in the family.*

This explained the forty-year-old elephant we had tripped over each time we shared the same space.

Illustration: I Know I drove my parent's to drink.

"The elephant in the room is a dance around the unspoken truths. The dance becomes a collision of two lives which have spun out of control until one or both hit a wall they cannot pass through. The truth must come out to shed light on the invisible elephant if there is to be any hope for freedom." TSW 54

After this visit, my mother and I were at a great impasse. With much consideration, I put pen to paper and began writing Mom a letter to counter her blurt. I saw this as an opportunity to release years of unspoken frustration as I expressed my concerns of her recent trip. I was proud of the many versions that declared my pent-up history, but my husband Curtis saw them as possible bridge burners, not opened gates. Six weeks later, many renditions whittled down from eight pages to three, my husband approved my account of Mom's visit. Much to my chagrin, I heeded his counsel even though I felt the three-pages minimized my exposition. Perturbed, I stamped and mailed my bewildered response.

Within days, I received a solemn phone call from Mom. Her tone indicated she'd read my letter, "Do you have a minute?"

"Of course I do." I was on the edge of my seat. I waited for her to be defensive, tell me I exaggerated, or that I take life too seriously, or even worse, tell me how much I hurt her.

Without pause, Mom apologized with sincerity. She had no recollection of the unrealistic accusation. She was certain she didn't mean it the way it sounded, but in view of its content and the fact that there were witnesses, she didn't argue or defend herself. She accepted it. Further, she said, "Your letter brought to my attention perhaps some unresolved matters of my own and maybe I need to consider counseling." Wow. I couldn't believe my ears. My heart leapt.

I reflected on my husband's wisdom as it turned out my letter wasn't inadequate after all. Perhaps enough was said to open the gate of hopeful repair rather than burn down what was left of the bridge between Connecticut and California.

Without wasting time, Mom sought counseling and asked if I'd be willing to have a three-way session over the phone coast to coast. Of course I said yes, I would have been foolish to dig in my heels and insist it was her problem, not mine. Instead, I was more interested in mending three thousand mile fences.

Mom made the appointment and I had to trust her portrayal of our mother-daughter relationship to her male counselor who didn't know me at all. Forty-years old and twenty years since Mom left Connecticut to be with her mother, we braced ourselves to begin dissolving the invisible elephant that had been taking up space for far too long.

February 2004 my phone rang. Mom introduced me to the faceless counselor in California. Counseling, Ma Bell style, was awkward because I couldn't see the eyes and mannerisms of Mom nor of the man who asked me preliminary questions. Because we didn't see eye to eye on much of our history, the purpose of this session was to begin to shed light on distorted views of our past.

Once the pleasantries and introductions were over the counselor inquired, "If you could ask your mother one question, what would that be?" For a moment I didn't know what to ask, but then it came, an unresolved mystery that beckoned to be answered. I preceded my question by stating, "Some people repress their memory or only remember the negative, not the positive. Perhaps I've done that. Mom I realize you lived with an abuser, too, but there's something I can't recall."

"What is it?"

"Did you ever comfort me after any of the attacks?"

Silence.

Dead Silence.

Then weeping.

The kind that released unspoken sorrow laced with regret. Sobbing which expressed my answer so clear that I didn't need to see my mother's face with tears to know if she was sincere as she confirmed, "You didn't repress my comfort because I never gave it."

Like an archaeological dig after an ice age meltdown, before the eyes of our souls, the huge gray massive invisible elephant began to dissolve with each tear from coast to coast.

However, when we hung up I was left with my new truth. After the monster attacked, Mom never scooped me up or asked if I was okay. It was no longer my imagination but my reality. Once I finished absorbing this new ouch, a funny thing happened. I was released from forty years of uncertainty and questioning myself. While my mother's truth was real, I no longer wondered if I was forgetting something. As it turned out, my memory wasn't as faulty as I thought. The pain of her rejection became a moment of reckoning.

I hadn't realized I'd spent a lifetime unsure of myself, lacking confidence in my choices and person. Sure, I managed okay and of course made decisions, held jobs, am organized and reliable, but something deeper within my soul seemed, with reservation, to hold me back from bursting forth and declaring "Here I am world!"

My mother's honesty was a gift. The freedom I received from the truth of her absence released me from a lie that had held me in bondage all those years with a stifling grip. I began giving birth to a new me as I became more confident and certain in my decisions.

> ...the truth of my mother's
> absence released me from a lie...

In poetic fashion, this also released my mother from a lie that had held her in bondage. She learned a lot about herself in addition to how she was transferring inappropriate roles onto me throughout my childhood. Mom discovered that she too had her own internal housekeeping to clean up and deal with.

Because of my mother's blindsided accusation that started this whole thing, an unexpected series of events were put into motion that would begin to salvage what could have been a disaster. Mom sought further counseling and called both my sister and brother to apologize with true sincerity for things about our past.

My mother has told all of us how sorry she is and how she so wished she could do our childhood all over again. She herself has said she doesn't deserve the Mother of the Year award, but more than anything she hopes we can forgive her.

Our husbands were rooting us on. Now that it appeared we might have a chance to mend some fences, they urged us to visit face to face. Gulp! I wasn't ready to be in the same room with her since she left Connecticut two months earlier. Why ruin a good thing so soon after our victory. I'd longed to be looked at as her little girl whom she was proud of, not like we were competing, but I wasn't convinced that was going to happen. We may've experienced a breakthrough, but that didn't mean the elephant was fully melted. But I lost; I was shipped off to California.

March of 2004, two months after our Vermont trip, Mom picked me up at San Diego airport. We greeted each other with optimistic willingness, love and huge hugs. We both hoped the visit would provide the opportunity to begin breaking down walls of hurt, confusion, pain, distrust and blame built with years of mortar.

Tired from a long day of changing planes, I shoved my bags into the corner of their guest room. A vase of beautiful flowers beckoned me so I walked over and smelled them. A clear plastic prong held one of those little cards. Curious, I read the note. Paused and read again. Paused and read again. The tiny card held few words, but words that yearned to start all over again.

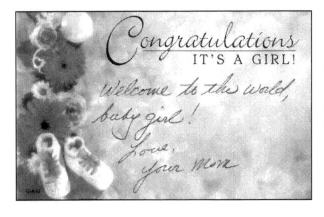

Congratulations
It's a girl!
Welcome to the
world, baby girl!
Love, your mom

TWENTY-EIGHT

Sweet Forgiveness

What does it look like?

I love a dry sunny day when the sky is bluebell perfect. The whisper of clouds give a hint of depth as they effortlessly hang in the air, the air that comforts me and allows my body to breathe without thought. My body seems to say, *Ahhhhhh I'm home*, as it heaves a sigh of contented satisfaction for having received this rare day and recognizing the blessing of it. Everything around me seems perfect and aglow with the richness of bright summer colors. Left with a surreal sense that this cannot be real, I want to stay on my mountaintop forever, but I know I'll have to hike down eventually. Deep rich blue hydrangeas are nestled near polka dot pink & white floret bushes, deep velvet purple torenias hang in pots surrounded by succulent-like green ivy, while sage with lilac colors are free to poke up from the dirt. Queen Anne's lace gracefully waves to the mauve hydrangea. Purple summer phlox, breathless white, black-eyed Susan's, wisps of angel white, dapples of potted annual flowers boasting their summer colors. I sat in my wicker chair on our brick patio and took in the beauty that surrounded me.

Our 1879 colonial home presented a backdrop to this new-age Monet garden painting. Every couple of hours a symphony of backyard birds sang their summer melodies. They flit in rhythmic frenzy to and fro, the feeders filled with sunflower seeds and thistle. With determination to survive, every movement is calculated, guarded and timed with the heartbeat of all the garden activity. My heart was at peace.

Can I forgive fears?

There was nothing under my bed, yet I feared being grabbed, pushed or dragged. Fear turned on the lights and gripped any stair railing tight. My fears reflected back to me what I needed to forgive. I didn't need to forgive the dark, but rather what made me afraid of the dark, lack of trust and security. How did I do that? I stopped feeding the fear daily. It wasn't necessarily a conscious effort, but a determined one for things to be different. One day I realized I walked down a flight of stairs and hadn't held the railing and I walked down the dark basement stairs before turning on the light. Was forgiveness melting my fear?

Try to enjoy food without the fear of getting more, getting fat, wasting food, wasting money, or sillier, if I ate every morsel on my plate China might not starve. By age twenty-nine, dinner out with my boyfriend Curtis, I couldn't finish my meal. Usually a frugal fan of leftovers, the guilt challenged me, but I looked at the plate, then the waiter and said, "Take it away!" It was hard, but what a victorious step. From then on, any food not worthy of leftovers has been scraped into the garbage, guilt free.

How do I forgive an old wound? During our courtship when Curtis approached to hug me, on auto-pilot my hand went up to guard my face. Curtis asked, "What's wrong with you?"

"Nothing, what do you mean?"

"You act as if I'm going to hit you."

Unaware, I flinched every time a person raised their hand. Curtis' honest observation shed light on something alive in me that needed to die. As our relationship grew, his reliable love provided a stable trust. I don't know what came first, my need to forgive or that he was reliable, but I do know this, one day I stopped flinching.

The weeping of forgiveness . . . was the day my three-month-old niece lay cradled in my arms for the first time. I was a young woman in my early thirties when I'd become transported on a wave of emotions. My niece was born on December 19, the same birthday as my deceased sister. The day I realized I was the oldest sibling with a duty to protect was moving day. The last time I held my three-month-old baby sister was when I carried her to the car. I looked at my niece and was struck with awe at the irony. There I was, an adult, holding this fragile bundle, so tiny and sweet. What must that have looked like for me when I was seven? I wept in silence with dry tears as I realized I was only a child when I found my sister dead and that there was nothing different I could have done. I wept for the loss of her, for my mother who lost her baby girl and for the sadness our family met that day. As if applying balm on an old wound that must heal, I was released from something that wasn't mine to own. I wept for the joy of hope to move on.

Can forgiveness restore?
Estranged from Dad's relatives, we lived separate lives as we each carried on variations of the family strain. That was until Uncle Gene called out of the blue to tell me

Dad was in the hospital. When my uncle called me for the first time, no warm fuzzy surfaced because at age twenty-eight, I only knew him as an extension of my dad.

Regardless, one day the cousins started reaching out to each other with a need to reconnect and mend old family fences that had been broken, not by our hands. Invitations to weddings, baby showers and dedications, and Uncle Gene's November birthday invited us back into each other's lives. Healing started to incubate.

We received quirky Christmas gifts from Uncle Gene: garden tools, winter gloves, a solar radio. He revealed, "I want to make up for the absence of my brother in your lives."

When Curtis and I married in 1996, my dad who had been dead four years wasn't available to walk me down the aisle. My heart urged me to take a risk and ask Uncle Gene if he would. Without hesitation, he said, "I'd be honored." I glowed as I looked at this man, whose features and mannerisms resembled my dad. Without mistake or doubt, a sense of family connection rooted me. Although my husband never met my dad he was able to see that side of our family beginning to make amends. To be able to ask and accept my uncle's arm was my way of forgiving my dad for how he discarded me. I could have been stubborn with my wound and dug my heels in, but instead, my willing heart unwrapped His gift of restoration.

Uncle Gene's aisle walk was a gift for both of us.

It was packed with forgiveness, regret, honor, sincerity, love, truth, family and effort. And a walk that, for but a tiny moment, gave me a glimpse of what it might have been like had it been my dad.

Can forgiveness comfort?

After my ten-year-old brother moved to California, random visits reminded us we were related. When Mom and I began dissolving our elephant in March of 2004 that was the same year Michael revealed to me what he experienced while living in Connecticut with our dad. We sat on the wall of a California gas station while Mike's car was being repaired. He reminded me that he was eight when our parents divorced, so prior to moving, he'd spend his weekend visitations with Dad at any one of the local pubs. Mike learned fast to decline a handful of quarters some do-gooder tried to give him to play the pinball machines. Dad had drilled into him, "Never accept money from anyone."

During one of those father and son outings the owner of the pub took pity on Mike and tried handing him a fist full of quarters. Out of obedient fear, he continued to decline this sympathy gift. Across the room from the bar stool, he felt the cold breeze of Dad's glare. Determined not to meet Dad's wrath of the hour, he was confident he did the right thing. Unwittingly he made the wrong choice. Once home, Dad laid into him, "Never embarrass me like that again. When someone offers you a gift, take it!"

It never occurred to me that he was having weekend visitations. The sickness of our family disease had cast a shroud over everyone in preparation for our burial. The only problem was we were being buried alive.

> The sickness of our family disease had cast a shroud over everyone in preparation for our burial.

Still waiting for his car, I was curious what it was like for him when he had been sent back to Connecticut to live with Dad. He shared, "Well, Dad convinced me that Mom didn't want me anymore so he wouldn't let me call her. It wasn't till years later when I learned a different story from her. Let me tell ya it wasn't all that much fun livin' with him. Like the time I played tree tag with some buddies, I fell and twisted my ankle but my instincts told me not to expect any sympathy from Dad."

"What happened when he found out?"

"He handed me an ace bandage, a pair of crutches and told me to deal with it."

Mike told me that he reinjured his ankle as an adult and the doctor told him the x-rays revealed an old injury showing he broke his ankle when he was young.

This was starting to sound familiar to my upbringing. At age nine when I'd broken my wrist in a neighbor's barn, I was afraid to tell Dad how I got hurt because I didn't know if I'd get in trouble for playing or for falling and hurting myself so I lied and said I tripped. I ended up with a cast. I can only imagine the pain my brother was in when he went to school on a broken ankle without medical attention.

I asked, "Did Dad hit you?"

"Oh yeah all the time."

How could that be? This was during the time I was building a relationship with Dad and his wife. How could I have not known? Because, this is how clever a lie can be that is determined to hide the truth. The smoke screen slowly chokes out life while haziness settles in; casting a cloudy film over what little brightness is left.

> ...that's how clever
> a lie can be.

"Well did Dad's wife ever put him in his place? I remember when I first met her she claimed she wouldn't put up with his bull."

"Ah, not exactly."

"Are you tellin' me she hit you too?"

"Well, for example, in the middle of the night she dragged me out of bed. I woke up to her feet kicking my head and back and she just wouldn't stop. I guess that wasn't enough because she grabbed my hair and started banging my head against the floor."

"What on earth for?"

"Because somethin' happened in the neighborhood they assumed I did it."

"Oh and this was such a mature way of asking you about it."

I couldn't believe my ears. I wondered how many drinks it took for the adults to come to that inconclusive allegation. My brother and I were on a roll so I had to ask if he knew why he ended up at the halfway house.

"I was told because our neighbor's house was vandalized."

"How does this get you dragged off to a halfway house?"

"I dunno, Dad and what's her name insisted somehow I did it while I was at school."

"What'd your neighbor think?"

"They wouldn't let me talk to him. All I know is when I stepped off the bus my clothes were in garbage bags on the porch and I was told 'Get in the car. We're taking you away.' Oh, and they wouldn't let me grab Teddy or my books either."

When Dad dropped Michael off at the halfway house, his action shouted you are no longer welcome and I disown you. As he turned his son over to the State of Connecticut, his parting words declared, "I'm done with you!"

I was speechless. My heart ached for my brother as I got a glimpse of how two people's sins magnified the paranoia of their own delusion.

As I listened to my brother narrate the cold-hearted treatment he received from our dad and his step-mother, I was reminded of battles I had encountered in the castle of my childhood with this unfair king of our family's chessboard. Encounters like when my baby doll and grandma Laura's life size dolls went missing. When both my batons disappeared or when my woodland creatures crashed, broke and scattered. The king had me second guess every move I made and every decision needed to be calculated. When the king drew near to dominate, he'd crowd my next move. Often, I'd find myself in a critical position. Threatened by the undermining of this king, he limited any moves I had left. Trapped in a dark square, my knight never came to rescue me. Like my brother, our pawns grew weary of the constant calculating of our positions.

While the garage still worked on his car, we continued our conversation from the wall where we each revealed fragments of our discrete abuse. Neither of us knew about each other because our ages and locations put us in different time warps. How twisted is that? So I shared about the time Dad wouldn't give me my dog.

Michael fell silent.

"Tam, I'm gonna tell you somethin' I hope gives you comfort."

"Francheska was all I had to turn to when I was getting the crap beat out of me. She was my saving grace and offered me comfort during a difficult time."

My baby brother, now an adult who towers over me, continued, "I know it was a loss for you, but I hope you don't mind, she sure did make a difference in my life. Please know sis, she was loved."

With tears warming my eyes, I saw a piece of thread beginning to weave back together the fiber of our unraveled family in an effort to show redemption in the middle of the storm.

It was finally clear why I was unable to protect my brother from danger. I didn't know he needed to be rescued! The burden of responsibility that should never have been mine, lifted. I found comfort that the loss of my dog became salve for my brother's wounds during his greatest cry.

Does forgiving the wrong mean condoning?

The fall of 2007, I attended the funeral of my Dad's older sister, Jackie. Dad was her little Johnny. Following the service, friends and family mingled at her graveside. A gorgeous sunny day softened the edge of loss. I stood in a warm spot and looked around at faces I hadn't seen in forever and others I had no idea who they were. At this time I wasn't real close to my dad's side of the family, but I attended because us cousins were growing up and it felt right to be there and get reconnected. I smiled as I remembered being in Aunt Jackie's kitchen when I had helped clean the long-neck steamers we'd caught as little girls. Then my eyes landed on her. I almost choked. *What's she doing here?* It never occurred to me that I'd see her, but then why not? Dad's siblings had befriended the widow many years ago. After all, she was their sister-in-law. The same callous woman who beat my brother in 1986, and chose not to tell us our dad died in 1992, was the same heartless person who allowed his obituary to omit our existence.

I hadn't seen or spoken to her since my last attempt for closure in 1992. I'd been so angry at her offenses, I was unsure how I'd react the next time our paths crossed.

Standing here at Aunt Jackie's grave opened my opportunity to tell the widow how awful she was for the role she played in our family. It became my chance to remind her how horrible she was and unleash on her how wrong she'd been to side with the man that beat us. Who did she think she was anyway?

Although our past issues remained unresolved, my big movie moment with its great one-liners faded years ago because I had refused to dwell on her harsh view of us. Now, however, fifteen years later, memories that I thought were forgotten and no longer held value in my life, emerged from my depths. I was now faced with this unique opportunity to speak my mind and set the record straight. For a moment I found myself lured into old thinking stirred up by many years of grief.

I remained calm, collected myself, and walked up to the widow. Then I stood and waited for our eyes to meet. After all these years, I was, face to face with a giant from my past. What would I say? It took her a minute to notice me but when our eyes locked I said, "Hello there." She looked at me as if to say do I know you? My giant didn't even recognize me.

"I'm Tammy Sue. Remember me, John's oldest daughter?"

"Oh."

> My giant didn't
> even recognize me.

She grew cautious as it started to sink in who I was. As I stepped closer to her she stiffened. Bathed in my righteous thoughts I took a deep breath and paused. My choices of what to say or do next unfolded before me in a matter of seconds as the inner workings of my heart overrode my soapbox moment. I extended my arms and wrapped them around her. Her guard came down and we hugged.

The boogie man of this widowed woman now appeared sad and alone, frail and weak with health issues in a body that would fall over with the next gust of wind. I sensed she had suffered enough and perhaps didn't have the life she dreamed of either. Had I unleashed my tongue's verbal revenge at this long-overdue moment, I sensed she might not even know the devastating role she played in our lives. Funny, how after all these years, none of this seemed worth it anymore. I realized that this woman could no longer have power over me, unless I choose to regurgitate the past.

> ...unless I choose to regurgitate the past.

After the funeral procession I headed back to the house of Aunt Crystal, a sister of Jackie and my dad. There I filled his widow in with brief and generalized family updates using random photos, hoping to trigger a conscience. Once the pleasantries of this unplanned conversation waned, I could think of nothing more to do or say. I was not fooled by her shallow indifference to me while standing in my aunt's kitchen. Nor was I numb to the sharpness of her past sting that turned my brother's world upside down, or to the recent cutting words she hurled at my sister. For me, the past damage had been done and the chance to repair was beginning. Aunt Jackie's funeral offered an opportunity to forgive this frail ghost who with a whisper of condemnation would no doubt cry. I thought, *where I choose to let my thoughts of yesterday take me will determine how peaceful my rest is.*

It was sad that Aunt Jackie died, but it couldn't have been more fitting to be in the presence of my family's roots, which once hurt, confused and strangled me because of Dad. After the well-wishers were gone, the remainder of the evening was a reunion for our family. Uncle Gene, Aunt Crystal, me and C.J and our cousins, sat around the kitchen table sharing stories of our childhood. We grew closer as we discovered that none of us kids escaped the aftereffect the foster homes had on our parents. The remainder of the evening was filled with loving conversation and stories that bubbled and overflowed to the surface until midnight.

Can forgiveness plant seeds?

In the fall of 2011, C.J. and I visited Uncle Gene now weak with cancer, in his apartment. He shared stories with us about his childhood with our dad and their sisters. He also revealed how grateful he was to the foster family that had raised them. They taught him and my dad the trade of house painting. My uncle was aware that his brother had a rough start in life due to his hemophilia. He shared that Dad would run away from the foster family now and then to be with their mother.

For an hour, my sister and I listened to his stories and then his views on Christianity and religion as a whole. He also announced he was agnostic, he guessed. He was respectful and accepting of our Christian belief, as we were of his. He laughed and shared about the time a couple of buddies countered his views and dragged him to an evangelical college debate. Uncle Gene shared that his foster parents' philosophy on religion was divided, and that their inconsistent opinions confused him during his youth.

He implied, without claiming, that perhaps this seeded his belief system of no belief.

As we continued this visit with reflection of our past and regrets and whatnots, Uncle Gene wanted us to know that he was aware that his brother had been rough on our family. It seemed a little late to hear that after all those years, but on the other hand it was good to know that someone noticed. Then Gene reflected on his life as a father. With a somber tone he said, "There are things I wish I would've done differently. I sure hope my family and kids will forgive me one day."

It seemed apropos to share with him about my latest project.

"By the way, I've been writing a book about my childhood."

"Oh."

"I thought I should tell you because, well, you're a big part of my story."

"I am?"

"Absolutely!"

Lying in front of me was the man who gave me away at my wedding many years earlier. No longer big, strong and strapping, his body was skinny and frail as the cancer was winning, yet it hadn't taken the sparkle out of his soulful eyes. My uncle was still in there. The strong jawline, when he smiled, revealed the man I knew.

Our wooden chairs were pulled up tight to his bedside in order to hear his weak voice as our knees touched his mattress. Although I had a hard time hearing him, he had no problem talking. In fact, he liked our company. All we had to do was engage. Lightning flashed through the window as it lit up the dark sky, then the rain poured down while thunder clapped its arrival.

Uncle Gene's weak low voice whispered, "I have a question about your book. Is it gonna say anything about forgiveness?"

"Well, yes. My intent is to somehow weave it in."

He preached, "Because it does no good to hold onto the bitterness. It's like poison ya know."

I nodded as I realized that something about my project must have grabbed his attention. I never had a conversation such as this. He was a stranger who was absent for a very long phase of my life. But at this moment, close to death, Uncle Gene had imparted a principle he himself learned later in his life. Perhaps this was the blessing that he wanted to leave with us.

Soon after this visit, Uncle Gene was transferred to the hospital for palliative care for the remainder of his life. I was moved and challenged by our conversations at his apartment so I found Bible verses that correlated with his sentiments on forgiveness and bitterness. I then scanned photos of his kids, grandkids, and us cousins, matched them up with a verse, made signs and printed them on cardstock.

During one of our end-of-life visits, I walked into his small room which appeared smaller because his family was visiting. We leaned against the window sill or any available open wall space. Uncle Gene was propped up with pillows against the wall, the life of the party, ready to tell a joke. People were laughing and sharing stories. I leaned in and kissed him then handed him three signs.

"Oh, what are these?"

"Signs I made for you because of our last conversation. Ya know when you were talking about forgiveness and bitterness?"

"Yah."

"Well you kinda challenged me. Can I read these to you, do you mind?"

"Sure, go ahead."

Everyone got quiet as I prepared to read the verses. "Okay Uncle Gene, you're the one that said bitterness is like poison. Well, on your first sign, this guy Paul said we should get rid of all bitterness, rage and anger, brawling and slander, along with every form of malice."[55]

"Your second sign is about this guy Job who said one dies in bitterness of soul, never having enjoyed anything good."[56]

"And I remembered at your apartment you shared how you found forgiveness, so for your third sign, again this man Paul said we should bear with each other and forgive one another if any of you has a grievance against someone. Forgive as the Lord forgave you."[57]

After reading to him in his intimate space, I handed him the signs one by one. He looked them over and became sentimental as he registered the photos of his kids and grandkids imprinted on the signs. In between IV tubes and morphine drips, he continued to take a minute to absorb them.

"Uncle Gene, I hope you don't mind but I couldn't help but see a connection to your own words. Just sayin'."

He smiled, "Well, what da ya know, I quoted the Bible and I didn't even know it."

"Yup, you're a pretty smart man."

The experience with my dying uncle was a startling contrast from my father's deathbed.

Uncle Gene died in October 2011. His kids made sure we were aware of the funeral. It's not that we wouldn't have gone, because we loved our Uncle. It's that they didn't want us to be disregarded like we were for our dad's, so they made a point of making sure we didn't fall through any cracks. Not because they owed us anything, but because they cared. And because over time we cousins have discovered we've all been through something.

The reception marked the finality of the event. I shared a family group photo taken in the 1970s when our families were beginning to unravel. Now, 35 years later outside the Newtown Inn Tavern, Uncle Gene's funeral was the catalyst that captured a group photo that reflected restoration.

Must I Forgive ... again? ... seriously?

Again and again and again, even if I have to do it seven more times with every new morning. I thought when I'd forgiven something, once was enough, but it doesn't appear to be so. The beast wreaks havoc with no end, wherever it goes. Therefore, forgiveness must happen as many times as it takes.

After much time on my journey, this is how I've come to understand forgiveness. While a hurt may help shape who I am, to forgive the hurt doesn't condone it. Rather, it releases the poison that can hold me in bondage and stunt my growth. If I continue to drink in all the unfairness that happened to me, the hurt wins again. Perhaps forgiveness can shed light on a piece of my hurt to help me see it with fresh eyes. Forgiveness doesn't give license to the offense that took place, but gives me license to move on, free from the poison of the anger. While forgiveness is meant for me to find freedom, perhaps somehow it will also release the offender.[58] I cannot reclaim my past, but I can embrace my future.

So how many times do I have to forgive? However many times it takes to dress a wound and apply aloe to a burn until healing is completed. Forgiving is an ongoing cleansing that demands my graceful consideration. So I forgive one layer at a time, and as many times as it takes, so I don't wither and die like a dried up old apple.

TWENTY-NINE

Mother's Day

Written on Mother's Day 2011

Mother's Day has always been an awkward day to celebrate. A man-made Hallmark occasion which puts undue pressure on a population of women who, for personal reasons, have their own emotional scars that well up to the surface when Mother's Day appears pre-printed on the annual calendar. The reasons are varied, for some:

Lost their mothers
Never knew their mothers
Don't want to know their mothers
Their mother's don't know them
Don't want to be mothers
Could never conceive
Lost their child
Live far from their mothers
And the list goes on.

As a child, Mother's and Father's Days were acknowledged in obligatory fashion with a homemade card, a tradition that wasn't questioned.

Once an adult, it became a tradition loaded with anxiety. I had to remember to shop for not just any card but the right card, a card that said everything for me, because

Hallmark knew how to celebrate Mother's and Father's Days better than I did.

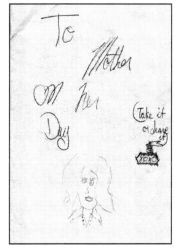

1970s card

Cover: To Mother on her Day. Take it or leave it. xoxo

Inside: If you don't like the looks on our faces tough cause that's just the way we want to look. Happy Mother's Day, Tammy Peterson

Now a grown adult with a disintegrated childhood complete with emotional scars of abuse and neglect, I wondered, how do I pick out a Mother's Day card for my mom who left the shipwreck behind? I was about to turn 20 when she moved three thousand miles away only to live near her mother, my grandmother, who had moved away from her mother, my great grandmother.

What type of card do I buy? Picking one could be an hour ordeal. I pored over the rack, pulling card after card after card, trying to find something that would be kind but honest. Many cards gave a variety of the same heartfelt message;

Dear Mom, Thank you for always being there for me, teaching me, loving me, protecting me, all the fun times, and on and on and on the list of attributes went.

Staring at my choices, I was racked with guilt for not gravitating with ease to one of the classic Mother's Day cards. The dis-ease of my childhood found me standing in the card aisle with unrest, unease, and discomfort. To add salt to the wound of this forced occasion, year after year my infertility, reminded me I still wasn't a mother.

Thank God for the cards with humor. Over the years my sister and I have had fun trying to see who can pick the funniest card with a wry message that best described our childhood. Mom's humor has received these cards with grace.

Still, many years since Mom moved to California, I'm saddened that my heart can't pick one of those thank you for always being there cards, because it would seem like a lie.

Sadly, the cliché 'you can't put the egg back in the shell' rings true when I cannot get back my childhood or the last twenty something years of living long distance from my mother. However, we have been able to make scrambled eggs out of our mess, or should I say, we're learning to unscramble the mess that poured out of our fragile cracked shells.

Over the years we've been able to share and express our hurts as we both rediscovered who we were individually. We have also accepted who we are as a mother and daughter, long distance. Beginning to dissolve the big elephant in 2004 (chapter-The Gift) was like unclogging the dam to allow some movement, yet I wondered why is it still hard to find a genuine card? Well, I discovered, the facts don't change just because healing begins. There are many years to sift through and much to reckon with. The challenge became not to let the old facts win nor let them continue to set my course. If I'm willing, new truths will be revealed as I heal one layer at a time.

Mother's Day at the church my husband and I once attended had a way of weaving in a live version of all the Hallmark cards I'd never buy. Their tradition would set this day aside, not only to talk about mothers and their roles, but also to dedicate new babies. I am a big girl but no matter how hard I tried not to cry, year after year, this day really hurt.

Once I tried to convince myself I didn't want children. But, now older, in love and in a stable marriage, we decided to try. My husband and I were together in this for the long haul. In an effort to conceive, I had to give myself hormone shots in the stomach with a needle. It's kind of funny how God prepared me for the experience because just months prior to my new routine, we had a cat that had become diabetic. During her end days, I had to administer daily shots of insulin into the scruff of our cat's neck. Because she'd been with me since I was twenty-three, it was one of the hardest things I ever had to do. She was my baby.

After practicing on her and oranges, it was time to stick a needle into me. I'd slowly draw out my solution using the syringe purchased from the pharmacy. After flicking the edge of the syringe with my middle finger to knock out any air bubbles, I'd find a new spot on my stomach that was not too tender from previous shots.

One day during this routine I pictured Dad in the kitchen of Kay Lane shaking and mixing his little vile of factor VIII, then tapping air bubbles out of his needle before giving himself a shot in his arm. No matter how mad I was at him, and how much I did not want to be like him, I couldn't help but notice the ironic resemblance between he and I. Although the reasons for our shots were different, I became faced with a twinge of empathy for what he must have gone through daily. He had tried to safeguard his life and I had tried to create one.

By the end of 2003, my husband and I decided the monthly rejection of the hormonal calendar was too painful so we stopped trying to conceive by medicine and thought if God wanted us to have kids, we would. Because my husband and I never did conceive, Mother's Day continues to be hard, especially for me, so we began our own tradition of skipping church on this annual occasion. We've spent the day however we saw fit. We explore, hike, hit the best ice cream joints or do nothing. But whatever we choose to do, it's become our day.

So after the long deep and cold winter of 2011, Curtis and I were excited to enjoy our claimed day off because it was warm and sunny. After a lazy relaxed morning, coffee and breakfast on our porch, we drove to Massachusetts and hiked Mt. Holyoke.

Home by 7:00 p.m., I prepped dinner, wrapped up a few chores, and was ready to call it a day until I looked at the clock and sighed. It was half past nine when I realized I hadn't called my mother yet. I couldn't call her in the morning, because she's on the west coast. I couldn't call her mid-afternoon because we'd escaped to enjoy our hike. Now that I was ready to go to bed, I could not. I had to call her so she could hear me say, "Happy Mother's Day" and then listen to her detailed report of the wonderful treats she received from her husband.

Tired and irritated, I called.

Mom filled me in on the cards she received from my sister and brother as I muttered, "Mine's on the way."

Polite she said, "I'm sure I'll get it Monday."

Under my breath I prayed, *I hope so.*

A grown adult and I'm still met with the frustration of this tradition.

However, we talked almost two hours.

I had told Mom back in January that I was writing a book. I'd already been working on it for quite some time, but didn't want to tell her until I had a solid grasp of this project I started. It had been a slow simmering pot because regardless of my upbringing, my aim was not to hurt anyone, most of all my mother.

Now five months since she learned I was writing she asked, "How's your book coming along?"

"Slowly."

Mom's curiosity about my book's progression opened a dialogue which segued into her own childhood where she shared, "One Vermont Christmas when our family struggled financially, I heard my mother crying because they only had ten dollars to split between me and Dee for gifts."

Noting a tough financial time for my grandparents, I asked Mom if she and Dad always struggled financially when raising us kids. "Yes we did, during much of our marriage. But of the nine houses we lived in, life was good at Washbrook Road. One Easter Sunday your dad backed his pickup truck over the lawn and parked at the front door. The whole bed of the truck was filled with tulips, hyacinths and daffodils. You girls help me unload them into the house. The fragrance of more beautiful Easter flowers than you could imagine filled our home for days. And the time when your father bought a used Cadillac, we thought we were moving up and had finally made it to the top. But then the building trade shifted and contractors could no longer get loans. Everything was at a standstill which left builders stuck with all the mortgages of the houses they'd built. And no matter our situation or what house we lived in, your father always had health issues, so yes, to answer your question, we struggled."

The Mt. Holyoke hike my husband and I took earlier that afternoon seemed like another lifetime ago as more stories flashed back and forth between me and mom until we landed on moving day when I was seven.

Mom shared, "I took Sandy to the doctor on a Tuesday for her checkup and he said I had a healthy three-month-old little girl. When your father came home I told him the wonderful news! To which he said, 'Good because we've sold the house and have to be out in two days. We're moving on Thursday.'"

"I had two days to pack up three kids, the house, and find a moving company on such short notice. I did. We moved. Sandy died."

Of course I'd heard this story many times before, but this time, a little older and no longer anxious to get off the phone, I listened to my mother with new ears. She then shared how she had asked the movers to pack Sandy's crib last so it would be the first thing unloaded off the truck, and the first thing to get set up. Forty years later I learned a different version of moving day from what my seven-year-old life recalled. Rather than being knit together in our separate pains, our family had been torn apart by the fraying of our losses.

My experience of that day wasn't any less traumatic or real for a little girl who picked up her dead baby sister. It's just that I learned there is always another side to a story, Mom's side: *A young mother in her thirties with three children, seven, six and three months old, and a husband with health and anger issues as alcohol began to magnify his own losses. She packed a home and kids in two days and then her healthy baby died. As if that wasn't enough, about a week after her baby's death, the photographer came to the yellow house, beaming as he hand-delivered the first professional photos taken of Sandy. He didn't know she was already dead and buried.*

This many years later, as a woman who has cried over the loss of not being able to have her own children, I began to feel for the pain my mother must have gone through. Yet I also realized I wasn't in her shoes because we never did have a baby. Softened, I was moved and humbled by her rendition. "Mom, that hadda be hard. I can't even imagine what it must've been like for you. I'm so sorry for what you've gone through."

In her indelible way, laced with ever-ready humor she said, "Well, I'm still here to tell about it."

I was thankful that over thirty years ago I had come to my good senses and apologized for the time I had blamed her for Sandy's death. She had understood it was a little girl's pain and the logic of a seven-year-old who was sad, but it was still a sting that needed to be addressed to let the air out of any false misgivings. At the end of the day it wasn't me or Mom or the crib. It was SIDS.[59] It was sad. It was heartbreaking. Our whole family had lost something on the day that we lost someone.

During the late night phone call, I began to see the strength and courage it must have taken for Mom to carry on. I wondered if the backbone I said she never had was instead, misaligned. Perhaps her constant humor which seemed to gloss over the reality of our abuse was instead endurance. Maybe what appeared as passive and weakness toward her husband, our dad, was perhaps love mixed with survival mode. Perhaps they were traits gleaned from her idyllic Vermont childhood.

Don't get me wrong, I had no peaceful upbringing, nor a mother and daughter relationship Hallmark style, and I certainly didn't grow up in a Christian environment regardless of our claimed beliefs. And it's true pieces of my childhood were painful, wrong, real, cruel and abusive. It's just that I also learned there are many layers to the scars left by the wounds and so I wondered, *where does my wound begin? With me? My mother? Her mother? My dad? His mother?* Today I realize my mom was, at one time, a young wife and mother who was in a loving relationship that turned confusing before it became abusive. Because of this, she yearned to have her mother nearby, so she moved. I considered my mom weak, but perhaps she was stronger than I'd given her credit for. She endured a lot with her willing spirit. She has continued to be optimistic and wants to be helpful. I find her amazingly courageous for supporting my book. Fervently she wants to embrace me in conversation and in spite of our past obstacles, she has continued to hold her head high and tell her three children how much she loves them.

She may not have always been there in the way I would have liked, but she is there now.

Perhaps my visit to the card rack next Mother's Day won't take me nearly as long and I'll be able to buy that card which says, 'Thanks Mom for being there'.

 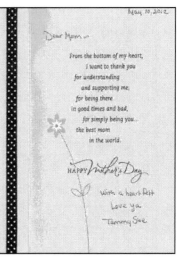

May 10, 2012 Dear Mom, From the bottom of my heart, I want to thank you for understanding and supporting me, for being there in good times and bad, for simply being you...the best mom in the world. Happy Mother's Day. With a heartfelt Love ya Tammy Sue

For you Mother, to Mother

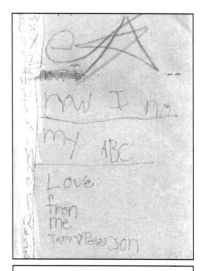

Now I no my ABC
Love from me
Tammy Peterson

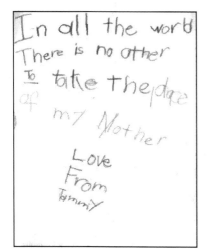

In all the world there is no
other to take the place
of my mother
Love from Tammy

I Love You

THIRTY

Where is Uncle John?

October 2011

In preparation for Uncle Gene's burial, Nancy and Bob wanted to bury their dad near his brother John who'd been dead nineteen years. When they asked if I knew where my dad was buried I told them I didn't know because the widow never told us and for all I knew, he'd been put out to sea. This initiated the search for Uncle John's cemetery. One cousin called another cousin and asked, "Where is Uncle John?"

"I don't know," replied the cousin who then called another cousin until someone found the cousin who could point to Uncle John's location. The cousin in the know announced, "I found Uncle John. He's sitting on his widow's mantel."

The search revealed that John's ashes had never been buried or scattered at sea.

The cousin in the know called John's widow to inform her that her brother-in-law Gene passed away, and that his funeral will be in October. She expressed that his family desired to have some of Uncle John's ashes so the two brothers could be buried next to each other.

After short consideration, the widow refused.

Although Gene's kids didn't get their wish as they prepared for their dad's burial, it unearthed the fact that my Dad was never buried, so they had to break the news to me.

242

What a wild thing to learn considering the widow led me to believe back in 1992 that he would be scattered at sea. I was somewhat taken aback, but then curious. One might ask why I even cared because a part of me didn't. But something else stirred when I received, what to me was, news of reckless defiance.

News that told me my dead father and childhood abuser sat on a mantel for nineteen years. News that revealed the widow kept my father all to herself and reminded me I'm merely his daughter. News that said, Dad wasn't buried, but perhaps one day could be. News that asked, what would I do if I learned he's being buried, would I want to go? Was the widow right, was I a bad daughter? Could I have tried harder? The sting of the past lay dormant until these scabby wounds reappeared and challenged me to navigate through painful memories without picking them wide open again.

Granted everyone handles loss and grief in their own way, but, I'm his daughter! I had a right to know whether or not there was a funeral, a ceremony, anything. A person dies for real once, and the widow robbed me of that chance to decide if I wanted to say my piece or make peace.

This crazy mantel news made me feel cheated. Regardless of my rocky relationship with Dad it was mean-spirited that she never informed me or my siblings that he died and never had a service. Let's not forget the obituary that omitted our existence.

So how many times can a scab reappear? As many times as it wants.

How many times must I resist picking at it? As many times as it takes.

As I remembered the widow's contempt back in 1992 when she had stated my dad would be scattered at sea, I ruminated over something I'd written back then.

What's A Father's Love To Be

You always told me that you cared
By throwing me a cold, cold glare
I couldn't do my house chores right
You'd let me know most every night
What's a father's love to be
An answer from a book you read?
Or maybe just the trials of life
Can love be given without strife?
You robbed me of my childhood days
By breaking me along the way
I thought that I could melt that glare
But you only dragged me down the stairs
My childhood gone and so are you
Happy memories shared are few
I heard your ashes were scattered at sea
Was the love you gave what you felt I'd need?
What's a father's love to be?
An answer from a book you read?
Or maybe just the trials of life
Can love be given without strife?
What's a father's love to be
When his ashes are floating out at sea....[60]

Dad wasn't at sea and never had a service. Rather he had sat cozy on his wife's mantel. I believe my history continues to shape me. The challenge is to not dwell in lost days, but to let go of the parts which no longer enrich my future. Otherwise that old history will continue to keep me bound in chains. And chains won't help to restore my life.

THIRTY-ONE

The Executor

May 2012

Seven months after I learned of my dad's whereabouts, a cousin called to tell me that the widow had passed. Upon digesting the news, I flashed on the mantel. Dad died in March a mere twenty years ago. Now what? It's a good thing I'm broke; otherwise, I'd be in chronic therapy and end up broke.

Pam, another cousin, gave me the executor's phone number should I want to call about the ashes. I entertained the idea, but Uncle Gene had since been buried back in October. Therefore, the original request to mix a little bit of my dad's ashes with his brother Gene was moot. And besides, I had also learned through the cousin-grapevine that the executor of these affairs became a friend of the widow only after my dad died, so she never knew him. Considering my experience with Dad's wife, I wasn't sure how far I'd get if I called this lady. What if she was just like her? The adult I'd become was capable of conquering the challenge. But the little girl inside of me hesitated because she wasn't sure if she could take anymore rejection from her father's grave, or should I say the mantel. The little girl who never received her father's blessing didn't know where her threshold was or how fast she would crumble should she hear the wrong words.

After some thought, it didn't take long to conclude, *what more could I lose?* What if there was a plan to toss the widow and Dad into the ocean? This could be my last opportunity for some form of closure. I took a deep prayerful breath, called the mystery woman, and introduced myself to her answering machine as John Peterson's daughter.

A few days passed before the executor returned my call. After pleasantries and acknowledgement of the stranger's loss, I was gentle yet succinct as I wove into our conversation how I had thought my dad had been buried a long time ago. She didn't know me from Adam, so the rumor suggesting she'd heard what lousy kids we were seemed validated when my report did not shock her. Frontloaded with twenty years of rejection, dismissed by the wave of Dad's hand, I was tempted to launch and set her straight. But I paused and somehow decided it was not my place to burden her with our family's history.

What a delicate conversation we had. She revealed some frustrations with the weight of handling her friend's estate. I genuinely tried to comfort and encourage her. Eventually, when it seemed appropriate, I asked if there was going to be a service for my dad. She expressed that he might finally get put out to sea, but in the meantime immediate plans were being made for her friend's memorial service to be held towards the end of May. I figured this was my last chance so I bit the bullet.

"I know you're overwhelmed and have a lot on your plate, but I need to ask a question."

"What is it?"

"This might seem strange, but I have to ask. Is it possible to have a handful of my dad's ashes before you bury him at sea? This way our family can have closure."

She was polite as she listened to this awkward request, but because she hesitated, the inside of my head screamed, *you have no right to keep a part of my loss!*

Some of Dad's ashes weren't the only thing I wanted. With this window of opportunity, I saw a small crack, but an opening nonetheless, so I lobbed another request her way. "Uh, I have a brother who lived with them at one time."

"I know, I heard."

"Well I wondered if when you go through your friend's condo would you keep an eye out for old boxes or bags filled with anything that might resemble a young boy's belongings?"

"Sure I will. How long ago did he live there?"

"Well, it's been over thirty years, I know it's crazy, but who knows what ya might find."

"Is there anything specific you're looking for?"

"Yes, a teddy bear and a Hardy Boys book collection."

She noted my request, but made no promises other than a willingness to look for anything that resembled those old items.

Once my verbal petition for some ashes, books and a bear were made and the awkward silence passed, the executor queried where her friend's soul might reside. After 20 years of trying to resuscitate life of a new kind into her dead friend, she couldn't bear to imagine her anywhere but up. She hoped God had answered her prayers.

I listened as she grieved the loss of her friend, my foe. We were each left with a different loss. Shaking my head on the other end of the phone, I thought, she doesn't know the whole story. Trust me, Dad was no angel, but his wife helped feed the discord. This lady seemed to know someone different. Someone we never knew. Maybe the widow had changed over the years. How I wanted to inform her of the mean and bitter role her friend played in our lives, but then again I bit my tongue because I have been shown mercy numerous times.

Forgetting the original intent of the phone call, the executor and I talked for hours about new beginnings, mercy and God's grace.

A week later, the executor called me back to report she hadn't forgotten me or my requests. She'd given our conversation much thought. As if a fog had lifted, she intimated that perhaps she didn't know everything about her friend's history and maybe some of the stories she'd heard were incomplete, therefore she concluded that the children of the deceased man named John had a right to some closure. I was very surprised but pleased.

"How much of your dad's ashes were you looking for?"

I assured her as the first time, "A handful, maybe the size of a small pill bottle."

"And can you remind me, what was the name of your brother's books?

"The Hardy Boy's collection."

"Oh, I know, one more thing, can you describe his bear, like what did it look like?"

"Well, he'd be over thirty years old by now. On second thought if I do my math right, more like forty." I thought to myself, his bear, Teddy, would be tattered, perhaps like my brother's memories, but holding all his youthful promise like a time capsule. Boy how I prayed she'd find him.

Our conversation was civil and kind. I thanked her and told her how much I appreciated that she returned my call, listened, and respected our family's need for closure.

Before hanging up, the executor informed me that her friend's memorial service was still planned for May at which time she'd hand over to me some of Dad's ashes. She asked that I be patient and assured me she'd call when the details were finalized.

After I hung up, I thought, *you've got to be kidding. You couldn't pay me enough to go to that woman's service.* That was an unexpected twist I wasn't prepared for.

I know, a little ungrateful attitude, but each time that scab is picked I am whacked by a series of emotions hurled at me. First the ashes surface and now, if I want a part of my dad, go to the widow's wake, are you kidding me? But it seemed to fit the lunacy of the whole story so I laughed out loud and shouted at the air, "And furthermore, should I actually obtain some of your ashes Dad, I have no idea what I'll do with them but I tell ya what, I reserve the right to do nothin' or with a final gesture, flush you down the toilet!"

When my cousins Nancy and Bob learned of the chance to get some ashes, they proposed, "Ya know Tam, if you get some of your dad's ashes, we'd like to offer you the other side of the double plot where our dad was buried."

I was overwhelmed. If I got the ashes, what would I do? Would I bury him in our back yard, use him for lawn fertilizer? Would I really flush him down the toilet? I suppose I could let him be buried next to his brother Gene, but what would they care they're dead. After all these years, I should have had the right to do whatever I wanted. Maybe I'd scatter him at sea so my corny poem wouldn't be a lie. All of a sudden many hypothetical choices loomed over me. My cousins' generous and unexpected gift was filled with love and an opportunity to let the dead lie dead in the ground. The decision to let the brothers, Gene and John, be buried side by side became mine in its entirety. My cousins' offer brought me closer and closer to my crossroad. Thank God I had a little time to let it sink in. Regardless of what my decision would be, I discovered that one may only die once, but one death might have many opportunities for closure.

Because of my cousins' offer they held off on finalizing Uncle Gene's cemetery marker which had space for two names. This left their dad's burial site unfinished along with their personal closure while they waited alongside me for the call that promised to grant me a handful of Dad's ashes. As if in a prison of my youth, I waited for the call that might also release me from a life sentence of thoughts whispering, *why-bother and you-don't-matter.* Regardless of what I would choose to do with the ashes, I remained hopeful that if I received them they would free me from the death grip of old old memories.

I awaited the executor's call....

THIRTY-TWO

The Executor's Ruling

June 2012

A month passed. Still waiting for details on the widow's wake my patience turned to skepticism. Concerned that the executor had changed her mind, I called the funeral home to see if there had been a memorial service without me. The attendant assured me it had yet to be scheduled. The funeral home is where the hand-off of old dusty bones was to take place. With dad's ashes hanging over my head I grew anxious and wondered if we still had an agreement. So I called the executor to see where matters lay. Greeted by her voice mail I left a message asking for a courtesy call to let me know, the state of my dad's ashes, besides the obvious.

Ten more days passed so I concluded she'd changed her mind. Burdened at the thought of keeping Nancy and Bob from finalizing their dad's headstone, I thanked their huge hearts and released them from their kind offer. I concluded, "Ya know, my dad's been dead so long, our family's mess doesn't need to hold up your family's ritual." In short, my cousins ignored my concern and continued to wait alongside me.

In the meantime, my sister C.J. and her husband, Bill, had been in a horrible motorcycle accident. They'd gone out on their bike for a warm Sunday ride when a young impatient driver hung a left, throwing my family fifty-feet over his car. They sustained life-threatening injuries, and found themselves in different ICU wards on separate floors. After some time they were put on the same ICU floor, but still in separate rooms. They were bruised and wheel-chair bound with broken bones and ribs. Our family tried to impress upon the hospital staff the holistic value of joining this married couple behind pulled hospital curtains, but the hospital's policy said no coed rooms. Well, we understood that until they stated the same rule applied for married couples. C.J., who is not shy, helped the staff rule out sex, in case that was their concern, "Really? Look at us. Do we look like we're about to play nooky?" However, the nurses restated that policy was policy. Heaven forbid they might have a chance to talk, eat and heal together.

After a week of being separated, they were transferred to a rehab with a shared room. That facility understood this married couple had a traumatic ordeal that could have changed all of our lives in seconds. Across from bed tray tables, C.J. and Bill shared or had oxygen tanks, wheel-chairs, commodes, walkers and crutches, back-brace, and foot-cast's for C.J.'s wrapped and swollen feet which donned her pretty painted toe nails. By the grace of God, they could still cheer the fact they had saluted their twenty-fifth wedding anniversary two weeks earlier.

After any given visit to the hospital and rehab, the hour ride home always gave me time to decompress. I'd been laid off, was taking classes to ensure a better job, searched for our cat that had been stolen and was trying not to give up on acquiring Dad's ashes.

Home from such a visit, I listened to several messages on my machine. I was surprised but pleased that the executor had finally returned my call. Her friendly voice sounded reserved when she stated she'd be moving forward with the widow's memorial.

The next day, after a cup of wake-me-up coffee and a moment to breathe and collect myself, I returned her call. She sounded upbeat and eager to let me know she searched for my brother's mementos but did not find any vestiges of a little boy. No books, no clothes, and no bear. I thanked her for trying, but the results made me sad.

She then launched an explanation about how my original request for part of my dad had unsettled her, which explained the delay in the memorial service for her friend. This woman, the executor, had never met John or me, she only held his remains. So it turned out that when I had called a couple weeks back and asked for the status, that spurred her on to solidify her ruling. She shared, "I want you to know it took much prayer and soul searching to come to my decision." I respected her candor and consideration for a request such as this, but held my breath through the suspense. She concluded, "I can't give you some of your dad's ashes."

Although my heart sank, it revealed the ongoing status quo of my relationship with Dad. But before I could respond, she interrupted, "I want you to really know there had been much earnest consideration to my decision." With clarity in her voice of one who had obviously given her verdict its due, she echoed, "I can't give you some of your dad's ashes."

I'm thinking, *I know lady, you just said that. Why are you repeating yourself?*

I still hadn't been able to get a word in edge wise before she announced, "Instead, I'd like to give you the entire box of your dad's cremains."

I was stunned and for a rare moment, speechless.

Did she say what I thought I heard? She assured me, "It only seems fitting to give you your dad's full urn so your family can have closure after all these years."

The executor planned to hand my dad off to me at the long overdue service for her friend, the widow. Unlike my original reaction when I felt affronted at the thought of going to her service, I learned it wasn't for me to know how the amends would take place and that it doesn't always come with an apology or a big red bow. Sometimes it comes 20 years later as an unexpected opportunity faced with choices I could either scoff at or surrender with acceptance to what was offered.

Perhaps if I accepted, it would offer atonement along with a glimpse of healing not only for me, but my mother, sister, brother, cousins, aunts, spouses, the executor and anyone else who may have been deceived by the ruse from our past. Somehow, it seemed like a chance for sweet restitution.

THIRTY-THREE

Teddy

June 2012

After C.J. and Bill's terrible accident in June of 2012, my brother Mike and I ate lunch in the hospital courtyard while we waited for C.J. to return from her foot surgery. C.J. and Mike were aware that the widow had since passed away and that I had yet to collect Dad's ashes. While we ate our sandwiches, the conversation segued into our past. Mike shared in rare detail about the day he was sent to the halfway house.

I had always felt like that day had redefined my brother's 13-year-old world. So anytime he was ready to open up I was all ears.

"When I stepped off the school bus, Dad and what's-her-name were outside waiting. I headed to the house like any other day, but they blocked me from going in and told me I wasn't allowed in the house anymore. They said they were taking me to a halfway house to live. I was totally confused. Kinda in a daze I headed towards the house anyway and asked them if I could at least get my clothes."

"Did they let you do that?"

"No. They pointed to three garbage bags on the porch and told me my things were already in the bags and to start loading up the car. I asked if Teddy and my books were in there and they said, 'Yes.' But when I started grabbing the bags they told me to stop."

"Ya gotta be kidding. What for?"

"Well, they decided to tell me which one of the three bags I could take. I wasn't allowed to have all three. Of course I asked if Teddy and my books were in that bag."

"What'd they say?"

"No, now get in the car." Then they drove me to the halfway house and dropped me off."

As I listened to my brother's story, I shook my head. The halfway house was bad enough, but to have calculated which bag he could take?

Mike grew somber and shared, "When I looked at my life in three black garbage bags, I realized, like my belongings, I had no value and I felt like trash."

I couldn't help but reflect on the history of the bear. Our family memories appear tattered and seem to have left each of us in need of mending our own recollection of secrets that we've carefully collected along the way. Some secrets were boldly discarded while others were put on a shelf with discretion to sometimes dust off. The secrets we could no longer contain were shouted from the mountain top for the world to know our distress, while other secrets have been stuffed deep into our reservoirs. And when our reservoir is stuffed with tattered secrets, our flow is hindered from sharing our song, our story.

My sister Sandra Gay, so tiny, innocent, and new to this world, had been given a gift from Grandpa Gay, a teddy bear. A silly little piece of material filled with stuffing, button eyes and stitched edges that revealed the shape of peace, security and love. Stitches in the bear's back closed up a hole that once held a wind-up music box. I wondered if Sandy ever experienced comfort when she cuddled her first warm fuzzy before her three-month-old body was taken from us in the bleak remains of that winter in 1971.

When my brother was born December 19, 1972, the baby's teddy bear was passed on to the new baby of our family. As Michael grew, the bear gave him a unique fondness toward a sister he'd never met and he named his special bear Teddy.

When my parents passed Teddy onto my brother, perhaps it consoled their grief while at the same time offering up a gift to the new addition of our family. After our parents divorced and Mike was sent back to live with Dad and his step-mother, he had brought with him his trusty old security friend.

This lost piece of stuffed material seems to have caused a sadness which is still in need of mending. Like the ashes, I wondered how something of no value could cause such heartache and sentiment. When Dad kept the bear, was that his grief erupting fifteen years later over the loss of his baby girl Sandy? Surely he wouldn't have thrown it out.

Before Mike and I headed back into the hospital to see our sister, C.J., we finished our sandwiches and chit-chatted about the widow's passing. My brother, now a grown man, inquired,

Mike and Teddy

"I wonder if Teddy is still in her house?

THIRTY-FOUR

A Crushed Spirit Dries Up
the Bones

July 2012

The day of the wake finally came. After an hour drive to my Cousin Pam's apartment in Stratford, I parked my station wagon in the lot and hitched a ride with her to her mom's. They wanted to turn something over to me before we headed over to the wake. Walking in with our iced coffees, Aunt Crystal hugged us hello then ushered us down the hall to her bedroom. On the hardwood floor at the foot of her bed sat two black cases. They both hoisted the cases onto the bed, flipped their latches, opened the hinged covers and presented me with Dad's instruments from the seventies.

The rectangular black case, lined with bright red-orange fuzzy material, displayed the deep maroon electric guitar with its multicolored shoulder strap. The other black case held a white Harmony banjo, when turned over it revealed a psychedelic burst of yellow. I was struck by the familiarity of these old contraptions. My aunt brushed her hand over the inside lining of the guitar case, ever so light, as if not to disturb its preservation. Her enthusiasm remarked how after all these years, the instruments and their cases were still in decent condition. Then something caught my eye. High up on the neck of the guitar was a pick tucked in the strings. I wondered if Dad had placed it there twenty years ago after playing a Hank Williams song for the last time. Standing near my aunt's bed, she was warmed with reminiscent thoughts of her brother. As I listened to her, I was reminded that this woman was Dad's sister and that the man who traumatized me was her brother.

We closed the instrument cases and Pam took one while I grabbed the other. My aunt's watery eyes lamented as we carried whispers of her brother in two black cases through the kitchen and loaded these memories into the back seat of Pam's car. As an afterthought, my aunt handed me a plastic bag filled with photos. "Here take these honey, I almost forgot to give these to you." Curious, I peeked at the assortment, but as fast as I opened the bag, I closed it at the first glimpse of my abuser's face. It caught me off guard. This would take a different head space so I decided I wanted to be alone when I looked at them.

The widow after all, was the sister-in-law to my Aunt Crystal who had hoped to find a memento of her brother to share with me now that his wife was gone. Boy, she sure did! A couple of photos would have been nice, but all of this was amazing and unexpected.

Mom had bought these instruments for Dad in the 1970s. Instruments Dad wouldn't teach me to play. Instruments the widow said she didn't have. It was funny how the weight of the nostalgia was heavier than actually seeing these stringed memories again, almost thirty years later. It was a victory. It was closure. It was a gift.

Later when I shared with Mom about the trophies I'd acquired, she flashbacked to the 1970s when she'd purchased these instruments for Dad. More specific she remembered him being pleased with the electric guitar he'd received for Christmas. As this memory struck a chord in her she stated, "When your father changed his strings, he'd leave 'em extra-long so he could pierce the end of his cigarette on any one of them. To this day, I can't envision him playing his guitar without one of his Lucky Strike's speared at the end of a string."

With the car now loaded we still had to get over to the wake. Aunt Crystal wanted to drive herself. We told her we had a quick errand to run before going to the funeral home. Well, it was really a treasure hunt. Pam insisted on driving me, in part because she knew her way around Stratford, but more than that, because she didn't want me going into that neighborhood alone. Together we set out on our secret mission.

Since I'd learned that none of my brother's stuff was found in the widow's condo, I thought of one last place to look, my dad's old house in Stratford. I know it was a stretch, but I figured the only way to know was to try. I was determined to contact the current renter so I'd researched White Pages online and learned that someone named Juan lived there. Within minutes of leaving Aunt Crystal's we landed in the neighborhood of my brother's lost childhood where there were no breadcrumbs for him to find his way back home.

We parked and stared at the duplex. Nothing was familiar to me and nothing warmed me. My cousin sat in her car while I stepped out and walked the path towards the two-family home. Although the mowed lawn indicated signs of life, nothing about the sparse stoop invited one to sit with a glass of lemonade. But here I was hoping to find something of my brother's.

I stood on the cement porch and knocked on the right door in anticipation of finding the last puzzle piece. I had rehearsed ways to introduce myself to this Juan. I might say, "After our family moved, we noticed something missing." Right! Like twenty-years later. Perhaps I'd say, "When you moved in did you find little boy things that were left by the previous owner?" Well that sounded stupid. I didn't really know what I was going to say.

After a few knocks on the door, no muffled noises, nor blinds twitched, it appeared no one was home. I walked back to the car, hesitated, and turned back around. After all, this was a two-family dwelling side by side. I knocked on the other door. A man with bulging arms and tattoos opened the door. At first he was guarded, but warmed right up with a welcoming smile as soon as I shared the purpose of my quest. His little girl, a toddler with black bouncy curls and big brown eyes ran cheerfully to his side. I told him I was looking for his neighbor Juan.

He looked at me perplexed. "Juan? I don't know who that is. The only person that lives next door is Shawnda my landlord who owns the building." I shifted from deflated to excited, when he said landlord and owner. To me, finding Shawnda was like winning the lottery. What if she renovated the building and had found evidence of a little boy left behind. There was still hope.

I thanked this man and said, "Great, I'll just leave a note on her door." I patted the little girl's head and walked back to the car. Pam grabbed a torn white envelope from a bill so I could scribble a message. On the backside I wrote a succinct plea, sprinkled a hint of intrigue with my contact information, and then left it in Shawnda's mailbox.

Satisfied I had given it my best, we headed towards the funeral home.

It's not uncommon to find old Victorian homes in New England that have been restored, resurrected and converted into funeral homes for the purpose of viewing the dead. These restored homes are a place for mourners to come and grieve the many losses which can no longer be restored or brought back to life.

We arrived at the funeral home anxious to get out of the stifling humidity of July. The Isaac Lewis Homestead[61] was renovated to capture the integrity of its era, yet offered modern accommodations in which to pay one's respect. I was relieved it had A/C. With an urge to use the ladies room before anything else, I walked briskly through the foyer and down the hallway lit by chandeliers. Then as if on cue, my body took on a tranquil pace and began to move with respect for the mourners of two viewings that were being held at the same time.

In the powder room, I mopped the humidity off my forehead and upper lip, fixed my hair, straightened my shirt, wiped and dried armpits, and popped an Altoid in my mouth. Once collected, I headed back down the hall in search of the widow's wake. The left viewing room was filled with grief, tears, sniffles and words of comfort for the mourners who overflowed into the hall. I paused and watched for a moment before I hung a right into the other viewing room which held more empty metal folding chairs than people.

I hugged Aunt Crystal who wanted to know what took us so long. She didn't need to be burdened with our pit stop on behalf of my brother so I told her we got hung up. Then I settled into a chair next to her.

A handful of cousins and a niece arrived at the widow's wake making this a family affair of eight. A little small talk, nerves calming and weirdness taking over, a cousin grabbed my arm, pulling me up so she could introduce me to a woman who was beaming and eager to meet me. After three long months I met the voice on the other end of the phone, the executor. This woman didn't have horns or fangs. She was a sweet, gracious, and willing person who had simply been minding her own responsibilities. We hugged and talked like old friends. She introduced me to her pastor and others who came to mourn the loss of their friend.

Some of the mourners shook my hand with traditional rhythm as their condolences repeated, "I'm sorry for the loss of your step-mother."

Choking back words of defense, I mustered a polite thank you. They didn't know that I never considered her my step-mother, just his second wife. Man, I still couldn't believe I was at her wake! While sitting with my family I observed the random mourners who came to pay their respect. I tried to see what others saw in the widow. I listened to partial stories that indicated fragments of her life; some even recounted how funny she was. A few tokens spread on a table by her urn memorialized her life. Two photo boards revealed a woman I hardly knew. Glancing at the mural of her life I was taken aback when I spotted a photo of Dad. It never occurred to me he'd be in the mix of photos, but of course he would, they had been married. My eyes scanned the board looking for more that might tell me something new about him. The snapshot of her life with my dad was captured on no more than four square photos with him. I stepped away from the table, sat back down in a metal folding chair and continued to watch. I just wasn't moved.

The executor approached and handed me a large manila envelope and stated, "After going through the condo I found a few things of your dad's I'd like to give you." I reached in and pawed through its contents. I pulled out one item at a time wondering if I'd found a prize in my flat manila Crackerjack box. Copies of his vital records created a timeline of his birth, marriage and death. Enclosed were twenty-year-old certificates that confirmed my dad's cremation. A little laminated card with a headshot fell on my lap, his driver's license. It struck me odd to see this. It never occurred to me he'd have one. Holding his license seemed to humanize Dad in a common sort of way because it showed him in an ordinary part of everyday life. Continuing to sift through the potpourri mix I found a little white envelope labeled guitar and banjo picks. I lifted the flap and poured out assorted colors of triangular plastic picks from when dad use to play his guitar and banjo.

Both his license and picks were things he handled and touched. I wouldn't be surprised if he had kept a pick or two in his wallet like most musicians. The ordinary human connection of these everyday things carried their own weight of intangible importance.

The executor's voice popped me out of my thought bubble. With a sheepish smile she informed me her friend Doug forgot the box.

Like Dorothy in Oz, startled when her house landed with a thud, I sat straight up and went, "Oh." Then the voice in my head took over. *Wasn't this what I drove here for? Why else would I be sitting at this wake? This was an odd thing to be told.* Like instant replay the voice shouted, *See! What did you expect? Why should you deserve it? You're not surprised, are you?* And on and on the voice ridiculed.

Trying not to appear pushy, I mean, it had only been twenty years, I asked, "Uh, can Doug go sooner rather than later to get the box? It's close to 5:30 and I still gotta get over to the rehab to see my family."

"Of course, I'll go tell him." She spoke with Doug who left with a promise to return soon. Thirty minutes later, Doug returned carrying the box. Without wavering he walked right past me as if I didn't exist. Cousins murmured, "Where's he going?" "Can you believe he walked right past her?" "That's her box!" My face flushed as righteous thoughts bellowed, *How dare you? I'm the reason you went for that box! My box! Don't you know who I am? I'm John Peterson's daughter, like that ever mattered before.* While contemplating how to be polite but interrupt his stride and shout, *hello, here I am, yoo-hoo the daughter,* he made a bee line to the far end of the row of folding chairs opposite where I sat.

It appeared this was one of those moments when I was being tested to maintain decorum. When I'm sure something is all about me, something inevitably reminds me it isn't.

My family of eight watched as the man with the box unapologetically handed my dad over to Aunt Crystal and placed him in her hands. Feeling disregarded all over again, I watched my aunt hold this black box inserted in a clear plastic bag now yellowed with age. Without removing the bag, she placed her hands around the box, almost caressing it, but not. Tears pooled in her eyes as she whispered, "This is my brother Johnny." I watched her mournful smile as she held her brother on her lap. I was humbled and yes, reminded it wasn't all about me. The man did the right thing by handing the box to the woman who at that moment in the room was the matriarch of us kids and cousins. She not only deserved that moment with her brother, she had earned it. As little children who had been taken from their mom and put into foster homes, they'd been through enough. When she finished holding her brother on her lap, she tearfully passed my dad to me.

I decided to take Dad out of the plastic bag. I noticed the seal on the box had never been tampered with. Hand-typed on the aged sepia label were my dad's name and date of cremation. I had been ready to accept a pill bottle of sand and believe it was his ashes, but when I touched the unbroken seal on this black box it brought to life that this might truly be him.

Now I was face to face with the box that sat on the widow's mantel for almost twenty years. It's just like him to hide out in the open with his unbroken seal. Isn't that what we do with our wounds?

> It's just like him to hide out in the open with his unbroken seal.

My aunt and I both remarked on how heavy the box was. I'd never held cremains before so I had nothing to compare it to, yet I don't know why I thought the box was heavy when a full-grown man's average weight could be around 175 pounds. The box was passed around to those who were curious and wanted to hold him. His whereabouts were no longer a mystery. Now everyone knew where Uncle John was!

All eight of us were at this wake for different reasons. But in the end we were all there supporting each other. I started to think wacky was normal. I was filled with gratitude and thanked the executor one more time before we hugged and said our goodbyes.

The dusk hours were still filled with the warmth of July. Pam drove me back to her apartment so I could transfer the day's prizes into my car. I tucked Dad into the backseat and laid his guitar and banjo in the far back of my wagon then drove to the rehab before going home. Some cousins joined me to surprise C.J. and Bill to help lift their spirits. The wake and the ashes were not topic for conversation. Instead we all engaged with them about their condition to show our love and support as they nodded in and out due to their discomfort and pain meds.

It was quite a long and emotional day and late at night by the time I arrived home. Operating on fumes from my third adrenaline rush, I unloaded the wagon and apprised my husband of the day's events. I was about to go to bed and crash when I grabbed the small black box and said, "Oh by the way, let me introduce you to my dad."

Two days after the widow's wake, Shawnda the landlord called. She was intrigued by the curious note I'd left in her mailbox. As soon as I explained about the missing little boy items, her tone became so caring and gentle as if they were treasures she herself had lost.

It was a shot in the dark, but because I sensed her genuine heart and concern for these sentimental gems, I had to ask.

"When you took over the building, did ya ever find anything left by renters?"

"Nothing that I recall."

"Maybe there's a hidden crawl space. An attic?"

"Trust me I've been through every closet. I hate clutter."

Shawnda assured me there were no hidden storage places nor bags, boxes, or trinkets left behind when she purchased the duplex. But then she got excited and said, "But wait, this is a two-family house with a shared attic. I'd be happy to check with my tenant to see if he's willing to look on his side." She made no promises other than to call me back to let me know either way what she found. I was jazzed.

Fifteen long minutes later our phone rang. I was standing in my kitchen when Shawnda reported, "I wanted to let you know my tenant and I took a flashlight and we searched his attic, but unfortunately we found nothing."

"That's okay, I appreciate that you tried."

"I wish I could've done more."

"Ya know Shawnda, you did. You washed away any lingering doubt. Thank you for that and thank you for caring."

Selfishly I wished she'd found my brother's things, at least his bear, but because of her willingness, she confirmed nothing was left behind.

I wanted so badly to find Mike's things, wrap them up with a neat little bow and hand him back his stolen childhood. However, as my own lessons continued to unfold for me, I learned that life doesn't always get wrapped up in a neat little package, or at least not the way I think it should. I also learned that my brother's losses weren't for me to resolve.

THIRTY-FIVE

Dust

A rag and yellow canister of furniture polish in hand and no matter my efforts, I inevitably miss something. Some days it seems this old house, where my husband and I live, spits dust particles on purpose. Like, where do they come from? And when it's woodstove season, forget it, dust is everywhere. I'm convinced the old windows and floors cough it up when I'm not looking. It seems I dust furniture, knick-knacks, picture frames, mirrors, molding and anything that collects particles that come from God knows where. The vacuum disturbs the dust that wouldn't stick to the rag covered with furniture polish. On a sunny day, I watch them fall like see-through snowflakes. Okay, like, this isn't funny anymore. Because our 1879 home has become part of our family, we'll have to adjust to drafty windows, minimal insulation, warts, dust and all. However, in an effort to live somewhat civilized and offer a welcoming home for our family and friends, I'll give it my best shot without becoming a slave to dust.

With a cursory but satisfied look around the dining room, I gave a final wipe-down along the wooden backside of the old tavern bench where Dad has been sitting in his unopened box for two months, since July. Because I still don't know what to do with him, I see it and ignore it at the same time, if that's even possible. But I am determined to enjoy my life and not be held in bondage by the pile of dust in that box.

It had occurred to me that my dad had never stepped foot in any place I lived. I never had the opportunity to invite him over for dinner and he never made the effort to get to know me as his daughter, or to get to know me as me. For the first time in my life of forty-eight years, Dad was in my house. As he sat in my dining room, I wondered why it took all of this to get him to visit me.

His twenty-six-year old "Have a nice life" rejection lingered on. Had I obtained Dad's ashes ten years ago, or only five, perhaps righteous tones of victimhood would still have spewed venom out of my volcanic releases. I might have vacuumed him up while dusting the house or scoff, who cares? With the wave of my hand I might have dismissed his dead ash as he dismissed my siblings and me, one by one. But it didn't happen that way. Although far from perfect, I'm not as angry about this as I had been at one time. When I retrieved my dad, his ashes, about two months ago, I found he was no longer the antagonistic foe but more like an inconsolable memory who wafts in and out of my presence trying to summon my attention, at the most unexpected times.

When I first pictured ashes, I saw light, airy, fluffy, floating. Yet, none of those words described my childhood. Perhaps dense, gray, death, silt, dirty, clogged was more fitting. Alone in the dining room with Dad, I pondered the heaviness of his dead body inside the box. I wondered how much he weighed so I carried him upstairs to our guest room and placed him on the bathroom scale. "Hmmm, sixteen pounds."

This once self-elevated giant of a man who created many obstacles in my life, who made and broke me, helped shape and mold my outlook on the world and of myself and who pushed away his family with anger and bitterness, now sat on my scale. His broken mountain turned to rubble; all that remained of his wounded empire. His one man war self-imploded leaving behind sixteen pounds of unused shrapnel.

> He left behind sixteen pounds of unused shrapnel.

This black box, now in my life, became my crossroad. What war I made of it was up to me. I could be buried alive under my dad's crumbled mountain, letting the decay of his dead anger suffocate the remains of my life, or with determination, I could choose to breathe and live alive climbing up and over the sorrows of my past with victory. I must decide not to let this box steal my joys of today and tomorrow. Otherwise, this sixteen-pound black box still wins.

Now that I had Dad's ashes, it was time to call my cousins Nancy and Bob, who had waited patiently for my answer. Do I believe the ashes hold the soul of the man who caused much pain in my life? No I don't. But we have tradition, the last act of connecting and seeing for ourselves all that is final and our family was deprived of that. With resolve, I called my cousins and accepted their gracious offer to bury the brothers, our dads, side by side.

My dad may not be restored to his original state of innocence before his life so dramatically changed, but I wondered if the burial would break a link in our family chain and set some of us free to begin their restoration.

Maybe we could celebrate a new life in hope.

THIRTY-SIX

Rootless

By Tammy Sue Willey

Too many times I move

Neighborhoods and friends are few

With each crack of the belt

Every smack from his hand

Our family ties torn

My spirit broken

My family separated by miles

Separated by values

My own womb is barren

I know not why

I feel rootless

I wait for God to grab me

To throw me in the dirt

To plant me

Maybe he's waiting for me to dig in the dirt

To sow

But how?

I'm confused

I have no one to carry on my name

Many years ago I prayed break my family cycle

No more abuse or fear or pain

My womb remains childless

I ponder my thoughts

I cry, I pray

More tears fall

Another year of seasons changed

This time a sprout or two or more

Break through the hard ground, which I am

Now – only now – through God's grace do I see

My own heart needed healing

Years of bad dirt

Need years of good soil

Now might I grow

I waited for God to throw me in the dirt

No, I was waiting for my dad to throw me

Now might I grow

My prayer was answered

The family cycle broken

God my father

Not my dad

Has gently placed me in His soil

I'm starting to feel rooted

Now might I grow[62]

THIRTY-SEVEN

Prepare for D-Day

October 2012

As if my emotional cup wasn't spilling over, the pastor of the local church my husband and I had attended asked if I'd be willing to share my testimony with the congregation on October 28 about growing up in domestic violence. What ironic timing as I stared at Dad who sat looking on from the tavern bench in our dining room. This was way out of my comfort zone. I mean, I never had a problem talking about it with friends, but in front of a large group? But I told him I would. The Pastor asked that I be respectful as I share my war stories, what helped me heal, offer hope to those listening, and oh, by the way, do this in seven minutes or less. All of a sudden I was sorry I said yes. First of all, how do I describe this and share how I healed when I'm not sure of the answer. I mean, I just finished dusting off my abuser's black box. Second of all, anyone who knows me knows it's impossible for me to talk in seven minutes or less.

"Pastor, there's no way I can do this in seven minutes!"

"Yes, you can!"

"No way, I can't!"

"Yes, you can!"

Even though I argued with him, I couldn't continue to argue with a man of the cloth, so rather than persist, I chose to respect his position, picked up the gauntlet and started to prepare. Good thing I had a few weeks to work on it because I became nervous, anxious and guarded as I realized I'd be exposing my not-so-nurtured upbringing to my church family. But as I continued to mull over this opportunity, I concluded that my experience would be worthless if I couldn't find a way to share a piece of me in hopes to encourage people to break old chains of bondage. After weeks of rehearsing, timing myself, whittling, and honing in on pieces of my story, I summed up my childhood with a twist of hope and was ready to share my testimony on that Sunday in October.

In the meantime, with C.J. and Bill now ambulatory though still recovering from their motorcycle accident and Dad's dust settled, it became necessary to find a date to bury him before the ground froze. Vermont Yankee roots or not, I had no desire to wait for spring thaw to bury the man. Emails went back and forth between Nancy, Bob and me as we checked our schedules against the cemetery gravediggers. Saturday October 27 worked best so we scheduled it. God's orchestration of my journey unfolded before my eyes as I would be burying my dad on Saturday and talking about him on Sunday. I couldn't have planned that if I tried.

With my church testimony outlined and the burial date set, I had maybe a week left to prepare for the big weekend. Relieved, I had a little window to breathe. I relaxed for maybe one day that was, until cousins started calling with questions about my dad's funeral, and what they could bring. Bring? I mean, I was working on something to say but I wasn't thinking past that. That's when it occurred to me I had to create some semblance of a service. I mean, I guess I had to. How'd all of this happen anyway? Why didn't I dig a big gigantic hole in the back yard and bury Dad along the fence line with the rest of our dead pets? It would be brief, simple and done. Why am I doing this? Because, if I let hope have its way, it will. Shy a week from October 27, my sole focus became Dad's funeral, D-Day, Dad's Day.

My siblings, fully informed of all the details, gave me their blessing to make any decisions regarding our dad so I wasn't surprised when both said, "Thanks, but no thanks, we won't be there." They got no argument from me, I respected their choices. My siblings and I are on a different time-line with our grief. If I've learned anything, it's that there is no blueprint to how one's grief will translate or how long it will last.

"Grief is like a chameleon blending in with the ordinary parts of one's everyday life. It hides well, then when least expected, its many colors come out sideways and reveal the day's new shade of grief." TSW 63

With my full concentration on D-Day, plans began taking on a shape all on their own. Emails were sent to cousins. And oh, I couldn't forget to include my childhood friend Dawn. No pressure. No obligation.

Because our household was negatively affected by the economy, I couldn't thank Nancy and Bob in the manner I'd prefer, but I managed a solution that fit the event. I reserved the gazebo near Newtown cemetery so I could serve my family brunch after the morning service.

My longtime friend Dawn called and without reservation said, "I wouldn't miss this for the world. I'll be there! Oh, I'll bring pumpkin muffins, too." Then my cousin Pam called and insisted she'd bring banana bread, cheese and crackers. Thirteen people had confirmed they were coming. Brunch was going to be my way of offering up a thank you to everyone who supported this unforeseen service, but had I turned down their insistent contributions, I would have taken from them the gift they wanted to offer. I realized this was a onetime chance for them too, so I accepted.

Then I received a text message on my cell phone which read *my husband and I are coming and I might want to say something, is that ok? Oh, and I'll bring juice.*

Oh my gosh! I couldn't believe my eyes. I texted my sister right back *I'm thrilled you guys are coming. Thank you for the juice and of course you can say anything you'd like, he's your dad, too!* Now there were fifteen people coming to what turned into a celebration of sorts. All of a sudden, this had become an event. Time was running out to finish writing my speech, sermon, proclamation, or whatever one might call it.

With D-Day approaching, I glanced at the black box as it stared back at me from the tavern bench in our dining room. To me it held no value other than traditional sentiment, yet I had grown fond of its presence. I became attached to a wishful myth about to be buried. All my life I'd been searching to fill the void and fix the hole that only a little girl's daddy can fill, but he blew it. And in a couple of days, I'd be putting in a hole, the very person who left a big hole in my heart. Emotions are a funny thing. They can laugh, cry and rejoice all at the same time.

When I had the house to myself, I pulled out the packet of photos Aunt Crystal had given to me when she gave me the instruments. Sifting through them, I revisited the man I was about to bury. A pile of 3x5 processed colored negatives revealed a Kodak time-capsule of his last 28 years.

The hodgepodge mixture revealed solitaire card games, beer cans, vodka shots, the square jaw. Holding and kissing a little baby and tender poses with children I didn't know. Sunbathing with his wife. Petting cats and dogs. Sleeping. Broken nose. His crutch.

The bar at the White Birch Inn.

Humorous photos of Dad, a side I never witnessed; stabbing the meat on the grill, wearing a blonde wig, placing a Christmas wreath on his head, or changing the light bulb dressed in only his boxer shorts and straw-hat. Many smiles I never knew he had; some at the White Birch Inn, a local bar that burned down, or a picnic with people I never met, and some rare snap shots of a father and son, my brother. Other photos of ashtrays and cigarettes between fingers while his linen shirt pocket revealed the outline of his lucky strike cigarette pack. Here was a man fighting his fight and a man who was old before his time. Glimpses of a man I once recognized as Dad reflected back to me the ghost of a man I never really knew. I sighed.

I pawed through more pictures hoping to find one of her. Although I searched in earnest, I was still caught off guard to see seven pictures of my dog Francheska. She lay comfortable on the couch or posed with Dad and the widow. Others showed her aged with graying muzzle. My first pet. The one they wouldn't give back. My brother's consolation prize. I sighed.

Somewhere in me wants to cry, but my cry is lost. Maybe it is playing hide and seek with the fear of being found and is afraid, if tagged, it will never stop crying. Maybe it will one day.

I reflected on a woman in the Bible who had poured perfume on Jesus to help prepare Him for His burial.[64] That was what her grief had to offer. I am not her, and trust me, my dad is not Jesus, but as the days leading up to the funeral became real, like this woman, I found myself in an unrehearsed manner as I prepared my dad for his burial. I had no grandiose ideas. Heck, I only learned a year ago he was still around and had retrieved him three months ago. I wasn't prepared for how this would transpire. I didn't have fragrant ointment to pour over him. There wouldn't be music or a minister making up words about a dead man he didn't know. But what I had to offer was effort.

> ...what I had to
> offer was effort.

As I prepared my dad for his burial, I realized I was preparing myself, too. I went to a salon to have my hair spruced up so the woman in me would be fresh and clean. I chatted with the stylist who washed my hair and for the first time in my life I said, "I'm burying my dad tomorrow." It felt funny to say that, almost like a lie. But as I sat in the chair with the salon smock draped over me, looking back at myself through the mirror, I knew it wasn't a lie. The young woman's polite condolences were natural which made it seem real. I almost cried. Along with my fresh wash and trim, I made sure I showered and shaved the night before his burial. I wanted to hold my head high, unlike the little girl in me who always felt fat, ugly, afraid and abandoned. I thought about my wardrobe, what I might wear. I was tempted to wear jeans, because 20 years later, why would he care, but I paused. If I'm going to do this, I'm going all the way, in spite of his treatment towards me. I only had one chance at this so instead, I laid out happy black clothes in preparation for D-Day. It was warm enough so I chose open toed sandals that exposed my fresh painted toenails. I worked on my speech, which kept changing day to day. Perhaps I was being prepared to bust out of my own cocoon and take flight to a new me.

THIRTY-EIGHT

Dust Returns to the Ground it Came From

October 27, 2012

D-Day arrived. My weather barometer, the open-toed sandals, indicated mid-sixties. The air was slightly cool as the sun hid behind the clouds. Not so bad for the end of October. A handful of cars pulled into Newtown Village Cemetery within seconds of one another and parked up on the hill where the main gate to the driveway led us. We exited our cars one by one and greeted one another with a smile and hug. People collected themselves in a variety of ways; they put on sweaters or coats, left a purse in the car, adjusted ties, pulled down skirts or pants that rode up with wear from sitting too long in the car, or because the static of the cool dry air made everything cling. Some grabbed their coffee.

People grabbed arms, elbows and hands and assisted C.J. and Bill, down the grassy slope toward a maze of markers and headstones.

Déjà vu. One year ago, October 2011, we had attended Uncle Gene's funeral. The gathering is much smaller for my dad than a year ago for his brother, but considering, not a bad turnout for an ornery guy who'd been dead twenty years.

Once on flat ground, my husband captured this unexpected event on our digital camera. Gotta have the group photo. All fifteen of us, I mean sixteen, if you count the black box, had posed for the family photo. Somewhat quirky but hey, these events only come along once in a lifetime.

Once the formal group photo was shot our family stood in a circle and shared random stories about two brothers who were about to be buried side by side. In truth, more of the stories were about Uncle Gene than Dad. Aunt Crystal cried about missing her brother, Gene, but then she'd weave in a kind story about my dad as she reminisced about her youth in a foster home with both of them.

One of the spouses recounted the one time he'd met my dad at a family wedding in the 1990s where he was fortunate to have met the Peterson's foster mom. Pam shared through tears the time she visited my dad at the hospital in December 1991, three months before he died of bone cancer. She laughed, "After giving Uncle John homemade cookies, he said he was getting ready to take the big walk up in the sky." Her words struck me because this was the most insight I'd had to what my dad's spiritual beliefs might have been toward the end of his life.

It was a simple respectful gathering. Nothing contrived. Some wore jeans, others dress pants. Ties, jackets, Capri's, skirts, sneakers, dress shoes. Everything shared was honest, some with tears and laughter. There was no mystery about the man who was about to be buried and no warm reflective account of his life. The truth was the truth. C.J. and I were both disappointed we couldn't talk in glowing terms as if honoring a life well lived.

My sister, who just days earlier was not going to attend, sat on a bench with her husband and pulled out a folded piece of paper she had prepared. We all listened as she shared her grief and loss through words composed from her heart; words that might put to rest her unrest of the past. Words from her alone could offer comfort as she empowered herself, and in return freed herself by sharing.

After everyone shared their sentiments, truths and reflections, I no longer needed to read what I'd written because they summed up my speech in spades, but I too wanted to be freed.

I felt awkward as all eyes stared at me. I shifted my feet, handed my lukewarm coffee to Dawn, took a deep breath and said, "First, in order to move forward, we have to acknowledge the truth of our past. This is what sets us free. If we ignore the obvious, we'll all stand in this cemetery avoiding the invisible elephant in that black box over there. All have shared at one time or other how my dad treated his family so my words shouldn't surprise you.

To me, Dad is a man who couldn't get out of his own tomb of anger and resentment towards the world. Instead of getting to know us when he was alive, he fought us, while fighting for his life. We've all faced many losses because of the ripple effect of our past generation's choices and pride. I'm not trying to be disrespectful," Then I paused, looked up and began my qualifications when cousins interrupted with tears in their eyes, "Don't you stop, you're speaking for the hearts of all of us standing here, keep reading."

I continued, "Some of our truths may be sad but they beg the question, when does the anger and bitterness end and when does restoration begin?"

Again, I paused, looked up and suggested we've been watching restoration as I said, "The fact that we're standing here today speaks for itself. Years of hurt may not heal overnight, but it can heal." More tears were wiped away.

"What if I chose not to unwrap Uncle Gene's aisle walk sixteen years ago? Perhaps I wouldn't have accepted the other side of his burial plot today."

Then I told my family what Uncle Gene had discovered in his last days about bitterness and how I had come to understand forgiveness. I read some verses from the Bible about bitterness, forgiveness, mercy and new beginnings, much like I had shared in his hospital room.

About to conclude, I shared, "There's a statement in the bible that's baffled me for years. It declares, 'Honor your father and your mother, as the Lord your God has commanded you, so that you may live long and that it may go well with you in the land the Lord your God is giving you.'"[65]

Rather blunt I vocalized, "I gotta tell ya this never made sense to me and at times it made me angry. I mean, how do I honor someone who abused me? It made me feel like I'd be condoning the abuse."

Heads nodded in agreement.

"So what I learned is that forgiveness and honoring doesn't mean one is condoning wrong behavior. After wrestling a long time with this verse, I've concluded that I'm not honoring a great person, but I am honoring a human being. Because of this human being, I'm standing here with my family today. You guys. My dad may have severely failed as a husband and father, but I believe more than once he tried not to. Today, I can't help but wonder how ripped off he too must've felt at the loss of his childhood and no doubt, the unfair hand he was dealt."

Aunt Crystal nodded her head in agreement as tears streamed down her face.

"Well, it's only taken me 49 years to be able to wrap my mind around that verse, but I wonder if forgiving without bitterness is what breathes life into this commandment. Perhaps making continued efforts to not swallow the poison is a form of honoring my father and mother. Maybe this is how I might live a long life."

I recited one more verse, "...and the dust returns to the ground it came from, and the spirit returns to God who gave it."[66]

"I hope by God's grace, maybe my dad will finally be at peace."

Then we headed to the gazebo to break bread. This wasn't a dress rehearsal, but the final piece of my preparation. This was the only ointment I'd had to pour over my dad's burial. I poured over him words in truth and forgiveness as I tried to make sense of our mess. By accepting my cousins' gift of the plot, I poured over him respect so he could be buried next to his brother. I poured over him a brunch reception for his family who gathered to comfort one another in hopes for a better future. And regardless of his dismissal of me, I poured over him a willingness to care one last time.

Perhaps this would offer new life through a kinder way of thinking.

I poured over him a willingness to care one last time.

AFTERWORD

Ask Seek Knock

Determined to break old thinking and family culture so I don't repeat patterns with a death sentence for the rest of my life, it occurred to me perhaps the fight *is* our family culture. It is what I have. It is all I know. But the beauty is I can change how I view the fight. I can fight to live dead or I can fight to live alive. "...I have set before you life and death, blessings and curses. Now choose life, so that you and your children may live..."[67]

Dad was right, life is tough. I just wish he tried to hang around and help me through it rather than fight me through it. So what did I do? What could I do? I guess I wrote this book.

January 2011, I'd tentatively shared with Mom that I'd been writing about my story for a few years. Surprised yet thrilled Mom said, "I can't wait to read your book, but I don't want to. Frankly you didn't grow up in the June Cleaver household and I don't get Mother of the Year award." Many times she stated how sorry she was. "I love you kids more than you know and if I could, I'd do anything to change your upbringing."

She became accepting and supportive of my new endeavor and offered to help with our family history and said, "No matter what, you need to tell your story Tammy Sue."

I was then inspired to write the Mother's Day chapter on May 8, 2011 the day of the Mt. Holyoke hike. I thought it would make a perfect last chapter because I thought my book was almost done. Therefore, I set a goal to finish it around the summer of 2012.

But from October 2011 through October 2012 I was met with many unforeseen obstacles that interrupted my plan. I didn't know burying my uncle in October 2011 would dig up my dad's whereabouts. Or that February 2012 I would get laid off a second time and our cat would get stolen for six weeks. Or that Dad's widow would die in April 2012. That June 2012 my sister and brother-in-law would have their life threatening accident. That July 2012, I would go to a wake I had no intention of attending, where the executor, a total stranger, would hand me my dad. Or that I'd bury him October 27, 2012, and share my abusive testimony at church the next day October 28. Or that my sister, limping during her recovery, would decide to come to the funeral and church testimony. Can I say wow?!

Through the pain and the healing, much was brought to my surface as I lived and breathed this book. Much of my journey goes back and forth between two small towns which at that time, many people didn't know existed. Therefore, during the heartbreaking tragedy in December of 2012, which put Newtown and Sandy Hook on the map, I could not help but reflect on my town. With respect, I'll share a childhood memory of Newtown before that dark day. No bells, no whistles, no tragedies. Just where it was before anyone knew.

With respect to

Growing up and into my young adult years, it became comical every time someone asked where I lived because their puzzled responses were often the same. With warm reflection I will always remember when a stranger wondered where in the world was Newtown.

"Where do you live?"

"Newtown."

"Where's that?"

"Next door to Sandy Hook."

"Huh?"

"Near Southbury."

"Huh?"

"Kinda near Bethel or Danbury."

"Never heard of it, what exit is it?"

"Off exit ten."

Exasperated expressions revealed they still had no idea where I lived. They couldn't picture where our small rural town was until I said, "The town with the flag pole planted smack in the middle of the intersection."

The light came on as they said, "Oh that town, I've been through there before."

With that, a smile would emerge and a hand might slap a knee. A laugh and quick wit of recognition to our town began as personal stories flowed about someone they visited, the sandwich they ordered at the Grand Union deli or the midnight snack at the Blue Colony Diner. Then there was the paint job they contracted or a delivery they brought to our town without hitting the flag pole as they high-fived their triumph over the intersection. Others acknowledged our little theater in the Edmond Town Hall when movies were 50 cents. Some commented on Ram pasture or the spectacular views from atop Castle Hill Road, especially during the fall.

We were warmed by painless-stories that recognized our once unnoticed town, the one with the flagpole in the middle of the intersection.

When I started writing this book, I wouldn't have considered my journey incredible. More like eating the worst vegetable I could think of. This was one of the hardest things I've ever done, but if I hadn't hung with it, I would have missed all that unfolded between my parents, my family and me and my husband, during this incredible journey.

I never thought I would have a new found relationship with my mom, now in her seventies. While my own personal journey is unfolding before my eyes, the same has been true for her as we get to know each other all over again. We've been tearing down the protective wall around our hearts so we can restore them one healthy layer at a time.

This precious time with Mom has been cathartic for both of us. When she helped edit aspects of my book, we continued to make new discoveries as old memories rose to her surface. To add a different perspective, below are some of the many memories Mom shared:

Memory from Mom: *"When it came to disciplining you kids, there were always three different views on how to do it; your father's view, Dr. Spock and mine. We could never agree so your father usually won."*

Memory from Mom: *"I remembered your father saying over and over, 'If you would only be stricter with these kids, I wouldn't have to be the heavy!' So part of me thought that if I actually was stricter with you, he'd be nicer. I felt like a wishbone being torn in two, with him pulling me one way and my kids pulling me another. I'm not saying this to excuse what I did or didn't do, but I wanted to share with you how it made me feel. He always told me I needed a backbone. The funny thing is, when I finally stood up to him and asked for a divorce, he said, 'I meant a backbone with the kids, not with me.'"*

Memory from Mom: *"I was constantly torn between who I thought I should be and what your father wanted me to be. I was his wife, but your mother. In your book you mention me as standing in the background doing nothing. I know it looked like that to you and I don't blame you, but I thought you should know there were times I was praying and calling on God to make him stop."*

My mom was inept in many areas, because truthfully who isn't? And although I've heard versions of these stories before, this time I heard something different. She was a bride, a wife, and a mother who discovered she was married to a man who erupted when least expected.

In my chapter, The Gift, Mom had accused me of being an independent two-year-old as if that was a crime. Her accusation had come packed with years of bottled-up frustration and hurts that she could no longer hide. Dad was angry and over bearing from his past. Mom was passive and somewhat naïve. Maybe it was their parenting skills and views on marriage that created the problem, not me. They each had to blame something or someone for what they viewed as a lack-of within their spousal roles. If the child-ness of me was causing tension between them, who was going to be blamed for their problems, the personality of who I was becoming? I don't believe my mother meant to blame me, but without words to describe the tension beginning to brew in our home, maybe that's what made sense to her. Maybe this accusation explained the root of the early message I received which said everything was always my fault.

"Then you will know the truth, and the truth will set you free."[68]

"Blame can appear immediate, but sometimes its eruption originates from the insidious web of silent lies that began to dilute the truth long before all common sense grew murky." TSW 69

The craftiness of abuse can creep into our homes to steal our joy and sound judgment until we blame the path of least resistance, a two-year-old. How sad for all involved, but how freeing when the root is discovered.

"And we don't discover the root unless we are willing to get our hands dirty and dig." TSW 70

May 14, 2013 at 1:00 p.m. I popped in to visit my girlfriend Sharon who said, "You look tired. How ya doing?" I shared about another lengthy online application. The process to find a job was like having a job. It had been wearing. Gone were the days of human contact.

"How's your book comin' along?"

"Slow. Some days are harder than others." My cell phone buzzed but I ignored it.

"Lately I wonder if I'm wasting time, like what difference is my book gonna make, but I have to believe God gave me this project for some reason."

Again, my cell buzzed two more times.

I continued to ignore it.

"Shouldn't you answer, it might be important?"

"Yeah, I guess so."

I flipped open my cell, read the text, then my jaw dropped. "Sharon, you're not gonna believe this! Listen to this, 'Being confident of this, that he who began a good work in you will carry it on to completion until the day of Christ Jesus. God won't give you a vision or a passion and then mock you or frustrate you. If it is of God, you can be confident that he began it and he will carry it on to completion.'"[71] I should wonder no more if God writes letters or can text a message to show He is with me.

In conclusion, the healing came not from hiding, but by asking questions in kindness and hoping for answers to be revealed in kind. Sure, I was willing and persevered, but some of my answers came because my mom was willing too. I took a risk by asking, but so did she by revealing. It took guts for her to admit she made mistakes. But I see now it also took guts for her to hang with the hazy secret of love and abuse and try to make it normal.

> ...the hazy secret of love and abuse...

The effort and honesty on both our parts has brought us much closer. Melting the elephant helped me to see her and her many losses with different eyes. At one time, her inflection through the California phone could push all my buttons and send me through the roof. Now I enjoy our conversations because I hear her words and tone in a brand new way.

When I stare at my pain, I don't notice the change, like staring at a pot that never boils. But if I put my focus elsewhere, the end result is the food was cooked and the meal had been prepared. If I had continued to partake in my anger, I may have never eaten the meal placed in front of me after all that time. I could have remained angry at my dad, my mother, and my loss, thereby keeping me in bondage and angry at the world. Instead, I chose to be curious one layer at a time. My willingness and determination to probe and question my mother about our past kept the meal fresh rather than going rancid.

Each time I asked a question and Mom answered, she gave me a layered gift of life. It was as if we broke crusty bread together, dipped it into the reservoir of our hearts and gave thanks to our old and tired bodies, trusting they would heal with peace.

> ...we broke crusty bread together and dipped it in the reservoir of our hearts...

Now, as Mom continues to encourage and state how proud she is of me, I feel her embrace, so I can no longer keep the torch of her neglectful absence lit. Today, I love her in a new way, and have found it in my heart to forgive her. If they give out awards to mothers who have the guts and courage to go through what my Mom did, then I'd have to say she does deserve the Mother of the Year award!

If I believe and trust that His mercies are new every morning, then I must believe He is giving me a fresh start to a new day to try yet again to get my day right. Therefore, who am I to be my mother's judge? If I get a fresh new day, why shouldn't she?

So after all that, who do I blame and who pays the bill for this whole mess?

During my search for blame, it never became evident who was at fault. But what I discovered was that when I'm at a crossroad in my life, my journey becomes smoother if I choose to look towards the cross.

And without someone to blame, then where do I send the bill? Who pays for my misfortune? I realized there was nowhere to send the bill because it had already been paid in full.

"He heals the brokenhearted and
binds up their wounds."[72]

"I waited patiently for the LORD;
he turned to me and heard my cry.
He lifted me out of the slimy pit,
out of the mud and mire;
he set my feet on a rock
and gave me a firm place to stand.
He put a new song in my mouth,
a hymn of praise to our God."[73]

CONCLUSION

Bye Bye

August 17, 2016

My Mother and I were talking about old family photos, which led to the pink sleeper I used to wear, which then led to the blanket I had as a toddler. She said my sister's blanket was yellow with yellow trim, a normal size baby blanket, but not mine. I had to pull the full size

blanket, pink with pink satin trim, off my bed and drag it throughout the house. Mom said she'd have to wash it every other day. As I listened, I waited for her to tell me that dragging a big blanket through our tiny two-room school house annoyed Dad to no end.

Instead she said, "You were so adorable."

"I was adorable? That's nice to know I was thought of that way."

She balked, "Why would you feel that way? How could you not know you were adorable?"

303

"Um because how would I know that? Dad never showed it. And besides Mom, have you read my book?" We both laughed.

I said, "Obviously I was very young during these happy memories you seem to have. But I could certainly stand to hear some nice stories of how Dad thought of me. He clearly didn't show this side of himself when I was older."

Mom sighed, "I know and I don't know why. But I do know it wasn't you. I think he had his own problems that he didn't know how to deal with."

She proceeded to tell me a story, "Your dad really loved you, ya know. When you were little he always made sure you didn't get hurt. I know kind of ironic now, but he bragged about you because he was so proud. When you were two or three-weeks-old I loaded you into the front seat of the car to take you to your first doctor check-up. I told your father I was gonna drive very careful like I had a dozen eggs in the front seat. Your dad said, 'You drive like you have Tammy Sue in the front seat!'"

Tears warmed my eyes at the thought of my dad actually being proud of me and more than that, concerned. Hearing that he cared, and that I once mattered to him made me sad at the loss of never experiencing this with him. But I was glad to hear that he had a heart and that he had really tried.

"So mom, whatever did happen to my blanket?"

"Well, when you and Cindy Jo were little, I'd take you to Grants or some five and dime store and let you see the fish and bunnies and chicks. You never wanted to leave so I learned to say, 'Tell the fish bye bye. Tell the bunnies' bye bye. Tell the chicks' bye bye .' You would say, 'Bye bye fishy, bye bye bunnies', bye bye chickys'. Then you'd be ready to leave. So when it came time to store your big pink blanket, I pulled down the attic ladder, then climbed up with your blanket under my arm and said, 'Say bye bye to your blanket.' You did and I don't recall ever having to bring it back down to you. I guess these incidents gave you closure. We didn't use that term then, but the effect is the same. Once you had closure, you were ready to move on."

After we hung up I reflected on our conversation with warmth at how far we've come.

Perhaps it's time to put my past to rest . . . bye bye.

ACKNOWLEDGEMENTS

I wish this list could include all the many people throughout my life who've played some role in my healing, but such as life sometimes we don't know who, when or where those people were or what seed they planted. Some people are from days gone by that we don't know the impact they made until we pause, breathe and look back. This is not all inclusive, but thank you to everyone who has loved, supported, prayed for me and mostly put up with me even if you felt ignored when I said, "I can't come out and play, I'm working on my book." **Family and friends:** In-laws, out-laws, aunts, uncles, cousins, today and long ago friends because all are part of this story fabric. To everyone who read any part of my book and gave feedback, all the good, bad and the ugly advice was invaluable. **Immediate family:** who I've fought with, cried, laughed, grown and healed with. **Mom:** although this project has been painful for her, she has given me her genuine blessing and support. **My sister, my friend:** encouraged me to write my story and 'get er done.' **Bill:** for putting his hand on my shoulder and for being a faithful and reliable husband to my 'lil shadow. **My brother:** who has persevered and maintained his humor while becoming an awesome father and has supported my book. **Nancy and Bob:** for informing me Dad was above ground and for offering the other side of their dad's plot. **Aunt Dee and Uncle Joe:** they've been reliable, loving, stable and a prayerful duo since I was born.

306

Mr. & Mrs. G., Mr. & Mrs. N. and Mr. & Mrs. P.: Unbeknownst to me, these ordinary families were divine interceptions that kept my course from becoming far worse while planting seeds of hope before I knew they were planted. **The executor:** She had every right to say "No," but her willingness to hand me my dad has added a priceless new dimension to our family healing. **Dawn:** my best friend since grade 5, who was and has been a calm voice of reason throughout my life. She hates it when I call her my guardian angel, so I won't. **Don:** my high school sweetheart, because he was. I'll never forget his young wisdom when he told me to beware of the jackals that roam around looking to hurt me. He was so right. **Randy:** We were eighteen when he planted a seed by suggesting I find new words to be descriptive other than say everything is pretty or nice. **Meghan:** whose friendship provided confidentiality when I took a risk and shared my first draft with her. **Rachel:** who faithfully prays for the return of my first bible, the one my mom gave me for my baptism; it was stolen around 2003 from a car break-in. **Allyson:** who said, "Just create to create," after I shared how stuck I was with this unexpected endeavor. It helped to unlock a dam. **Dana:** my text angel - random bible verses appeared on my cell phone when least expected and lifted me up. Divine interception reminded me I wasn't alone or being mocked. **Joyce Meyer and her ministry:** Enjoying Every Day Life. When I was depressed, she was the first person *I heard* talk about her personal abuse, how she healed and with God, all in the same sentence. Her authentic story gave me hope that it's possible to move past my abuse, talk back to the enemy and to not confuse my heavenly God with my earthly father.

New England Christian Writers Conference in 2013 (now called Renew-writing): My first conference where I celebrated my 5o birthday, stepping into a foreign arena of writers and authors. I was totally out of my comfort zone and felt inadequate. After I had a private critique session with an author whose words are Encouraging Words, I realized I was right where I needed to be.

Curtis Willey: Last, but not least, my husband, my biggest encourager! He has listened tirelessly to my woes and has been a voice of reason. He has been my port in the storm, stood by my side, defended me and most importantly offered me a *stable and safe place* to express myself. Not only has he brought music into my life, he has stood by his promise to stand by me since we said, "I do."

ABOUT THE AUTHOR

Tammy Sue (Peterson) Willey was raised in Newtown and Sandy Hook, Connecticut. Determined to make sense of her childhood abuse and figure out who to blame, her quest began by asking questions, digging up the past, seeking and knocking on real doors and those of peoples' hearts. She participated in trainings such as: Grief

and Loss for Women, Beyond Trauma, TREP Trauma Recovery, she became certified as a Recovery Support Specialist, and certified through CCADV to co- facilitate a domestic violence group. This along with the help of dark chocolate and hiking helped her discover uncovering the wound may not happen overnight but it can happen. She is happily married to a wonderful man, a seasoned musician, who brought music back into her life.

Photo: Calf's Creek in Utah
Barefoot-n-it with Barefoot Willey
one step at a time....

IF YOU NEED HELP, GET HELP

My book is not about minimizing abuse or any immediate crisis. If you find yourself in harm's way, <u>first and foremost find safety</u>, **call 911**, your local police for assistance. If you find yourself afraid, confused or with questions there are several resources available. **Call 211** (or whatever your <u>local info-line number</u> is). Seek shelter for safety or respite. Seek counseling through a counselor, your clergy or a crisis-hot-line, to name a few.

END NOTES
in order of chapters and placement
I referenced, borrowed and/or included a reference to correlate
with context of my story. Bible references are from NIV or MSG.

Dedication:
Epigraph: quote by Tammy Sue Willey
Encouragement along the Way:
Foreword: by Betty Ann Smith
Contents:
Preface:
Introduction:
1. "...protect me from trouble and surround me..." Psalm 32:7
Chapter 1: Tavern Bench
Chapter 2: I Hit My Head and Cried Today
Chapter 3: The Turkey Baster
2. I felt that my God was testing the aching of my womb (consider the verse) Romans 8:26 (MSG) "Meanwhile, the moment we get tired in the waiting, God's Spirit is right alongside helping us along. If we don't know how or what to pray, it doesn't matter. He does our praying in and for us, making prayer out of our wordless sighs, our aching groans. He knows us far better than we know ourselves, knows our pregnant condition, and keeps us present before God. That's why we can be so sure that every detail in our lives of love for God is worked into something good."
Chapter 4: Before There Was Me
3. Permission by Mom to share her five page love letter from Dad
Chapter 5: The Pink House
4. Walkers Farm School House - located on Hammertown Rd., Monroe, CT: was our first home. Per the Monroe Historical Society - this two-room school house was among the many one and two-room school houses auctioned off in 1935 to private owners. During its hay day, they educated 47 students.
This was our first home and would have fit inside the garage of the brown colonial my dad built on Washbrook Road.
5. Schultze-Photographer. "New Method Blood Record Set, In Massive Aid for Monroe Man," *The Bridgeport Sunday Post*, August 13, 1967.
Chapter 6: The Green House

Chapter 7: Aunt Park Lane

6. Sea of grass – when my mother read this part in the book she said the reason they could afford to purchase this house was the grass was so tall so the price came down.

7. We Say Our Prayers copyright1962 Ideals Publishing Co., Milwaukee, Wisconsin

Chapter 8: Moving Day

8. Joy to the World by Three Dog Night.

9. "She is more precious than rubies..." Proverbs 3:15

Chapter 9: The Day My Music Died

10. American Pie by Don McLean

11. Fresh Air Programs: freshair.org/history-and-mission accessed March 2014

12. From that summer on...bloomed for the three sisters to this day. Author note: Summer of 2016 the sisters visited and celebrated with stories of their first encounter seventy years ago.

Chapter 10: A Bowl of Onions

Chapter 11: I Could Fly

13. I Could Fly by Tammy Sue Willey, October 1994

Chapter 12: Play it By Ear

Chapter 13: The Lake House

Chapter 14: Serenity Lane

14. Serenity – Webster's 1828 Dictionary.com definition by Sir W. Temple/Locke. accessed April 2009

15. "A hot-tempered man stirs up dissension, but..." Proverbs 15:18

Chapter 15: A Bowl of Cherries

Chapter 16: Confusion is the Enemy

16. First bible –was stolen in 2003 during a car break-in

Chapter 17: The Grip of Confusion

17. "Fathers shouldn't embitter their children...." Colossians 3:21

Chapter 18: Will the Reign Ever End?

18. Darvon, a drug from the 1950s has since been removed for use

19. Field of promised peace and rest...references birds of the air in Matthew 6:25-28 and wild flowers of the field in Luke 12:24-29

20. September 2, 1979 TSW journal entry

21. ...my brokenness watered each shard... "This is why I weep and my eyes overflow with tears. No one is near..." Lamentations 1:16

Chapter 19: The Twig Snapped

22. A doe will sometimes protect her fawn if the predator is small... Whitetail Deer Suwannee River Ranch
www.suwanneeriverranch.com/WTinfo.htm accessed May 2013

Chapter 20: Pasta, Squash, Beans & Strife

23. Father Sarducci Cheescake – Mrs. G. wouldn't give me the recipe until I was in my thirties, and only if I swore to take it to my grave.

24. Since I was 15, Mr. G. planted his annual garden and always called me his bean-buddy. In honor of his deceased wife, I made him Father Sarducci Cheesecake every year for his birthday. Mr. G. passed away May 2017 at the age of 97. He was preparing his garden.

Chapter 21: I Guess It's Not Abuse

25. As if putting invisible armor on before falling asleep... (consider the verse) "Put on the full armor of God, so that you can take your stand against the devil's schemes." Ephesians 6:11

26. August 30, 1980 TSW journal entry–the barn/pizza

27. August/September TSW journal entry–he took razor and toothbrush

28. April 12, 1981 TSW journal entry–break up

29. "You drive the women of my people from their pleasant homes. You take away my blessing from their children forever." Micah 2:9

30. A Mansion, written by Tammy Sue Willey, June 2012

31. "Exploit or abuse your family..." Proverbs 11:29 (MSG)

Chapter 22: The Aftermath of Confusion

32. My wings were now clipped. Consider the verse–"But those who wait on the Lord will find new strength, they will fly high on wings like eagles, they will run and not grow weary..." Isaiah 40:31 NIV

33. 1982 TSW journal entry – parents finally divorced

34. Ammunition box –was stolen during a move in the late 1990s

35. Brett's spider plant - to this day I've managed to keep it alive.

36. 1984 TSW journal entry – Dad & I talk, miracle

37. March 1986 TSW journal entry – life outside of Connecticut

Chapter 23: The Hollywood Call

38. January 22, 1992 TSW journal entry - I pray for my dad

39. January 28, 1992 TSW journal entry – I ran into uncle Gene

Chapter 24: One Tiny Paragraph

Chapter 25: So Who Do I Blame?

40. BLAME: Websterdictionary1828.com accessed April 2009
41. Dennehy, Edward J., "Disease of Kings Hits Baby," *The Times-Star Vol. 147 No.5 Bridgeport, Ct Friday Evening* January 7, 1938
42. Royal Disease– hemophiliaprince.com/history accessed Feb 2016
43. Hemophilia -...mild, moderate and severe.
   National Hemophilia Foundation: Hemohilia.org accessed 1985
44. Factor VIII discovered 1937(includes Royal Disease history) according to PDF article: Kaadan, Abdul PhD & Angrini, Mahmud MD, ishim.net/Articles/Who%20Discovered%20Hemophilia.pdf accessed June 2011
45. Danish Letter Excerpt Translated Danish to English Dec 16, 1947
46. Danish Letter Excerpt Translated Danish to English Jan 21, 1948
47. Military Classification of 4F/Selective Service System- sss.gov/Registration-Info
48. Military Classification of 4F/Dating – NebraskaStudies.org
49. Ahn,Presca, The American Reader, Edvard Munch and painting: Scream 1895, http://theamericanreader.com/search/edvard accessed 2013

Chapter 26: The Fragile Dance

50. If seeds aren't cultivated in fertile soil, they risk being neglected and wasted. Consider parable of farmer scattering seed: Luke 8:4-15
51. ...and old gnarly roots that have hindered their growth need to be cut away. Consider the verse on pruning. John 15:2
52. I Stand Before You written by Curtis Willey (excerpt wedding song)

Chapter 27: The Gift

53. Quote:"The abuse from my past leaves me..." by Tammy Sue Willey
54. Quote:"The elephant in the room is a dance..." by Tammy Sue Willey

Chapter 28: Sweet Forgiveness

55. "Get rid of all bitterness, rage and anger... Ephesians 4:31
56. "Another dies in bitterness of soul, never having ..." Job 21:25
57. "Bear with each other and forgive one another..." Colossians 3:13
58. ... perhaps somehow it will also release the offender. Consider the verse-John 20:23.

Chapter 29: Mother's Day

59. SIDS –Sudden Infant Death Syndrome. Sometimes called crib death.

Chapter 30: Where is Uncle John?

60. What's a Father's Love to Be by Tammy Sue Willey May 1993

Chapter 31: The Executor

Chapter 32: The Executor's Ruling

BOOK DISCUSSION

Assume the word WHY follows each question

What made you want to read this book?

Were you glad you read this book and would you recommend it?

Did you find anything surprising about this person's story?

Did preconceived opinions about the author change after reading her story?

If so, was the change for better or worse?

How were you drawn into her story?

Do you have a favorite scene?

Is there a scene that makes you laugh?

Is there a scene that makes you angry?

Is there a scene that makes you cry?

What scene can you relate to?

Did you have a favorite line/phrase?

What do you think is the lie or lies of the abuse?

What are some of the lies unraveled in the book?

Can you identify with any of the lies?

What do you think about honoring parents who didn't parent very well?

How would you define 'honoring your parents?'

Does blaming ever solve a problem?

If you have recovered from rejection or a loss, how might you encourage others?

Do you think closure on an issue makes a difference?

Do you think you have to have closure to move forward in a healthy way?

How would you define closure?

Do you have a closure experience to share?

Do you think forgiveness means condoning the behavior?

Do you think forgiveness is a sign of weakness?

Do you think forgiveness is an ongoing process?

How would you define forgiveness?

Do you have a forgiving experience to share?

How would you define bondage or strongholds?

Are there things in your life that keep you stuck?

Do you believe in hope?

What does hope look like to you?

Do you believe that truth can set you free?

If so, do you think it matters how you reveal the truth?

What do you think gave the author strength to keep persevering?

We all receive messages, good or bad, from our youth that set our course:

- What message(s) have you received about yourself?

- How did that message(s) define you and/or direct you in life?

What do you think the message of the book is?

Where did the book take you to, if anywhere?

What, in the book, spoke to you the most?

What was your take away after reading Wounded Song?

If something stirred you, made you smile, laugh or cry, or eat too much dark chocolate, and you're not sure why, consider digging a little deeper and asking yourself why? Be kind and patient with yourself through this journey because it requires that. Should you need to seek counsel whether professional or with a trusted friend, then do that. Shedding layers is hard, but so worth it and freeing in the end!

If my book spoke to you or helped you, I would love to hear from you! Please visit my blog and share.

Blog: woundedsong.com

Wounded Song

Wounded Song

Wounded Song

Wounded Song

Made in the USA
Middletown, DE
19 March 2018